Fantasy Baseball

An Integrated Mathematics Unit for the Middle Grades

◆

by Tim Scheidt

GIANT STEP PRESS

Editorial Direction by Jim Fina

Cover design by Elisa Muñoz
Cover Photography by John Lei

Fantasy Baseball
Copyright © 1994 by Tim Scheidt

All rights reserved. This publication may not be reproduced, stored in a retrieval system, or transmitted, in any form or by any means, electronic, mechanical, photocopying, recording, or otherwise, without the prior written permission of the publisher. Individual pages designated as Student Pages or Transparency Masters may be duplicated for use within the classroom by the purchaser. Duplication of any portion of this unit for use in another classroom or use for personal, school, or district staff development purposes is prohibited.

Printed in the United States of America.

ISBN 0-9641208-9-5
Second Printing

Giant Step Press
P. O. Box 685
Jamul, CA 91935-0685
(800)475-STEP

ACKNOWLEDGEMENTS

Special thanks and credit belong to my collaborator, editor, designer, business partner, and most importantly, my friend, Jim Fina. Here's to all those late night/early morning coast-to-coast calls. Hey bud, we did it!

I also want to thank my wife, Dawn, for putting up with me living, eating, and breathing Fantasy Baseball for the past year. I love you!

Tim Scheidt

Additional Acknowledgements

Michael White, Steve Leinwand, and **Rich Crowe** for their professional support and review

Tony Spears for his professional support and organization of Fantasy Baseball workshops

Steve Scheidt for creating Fantasy Baseball flyers and his contributions to cover design

Kathy Bass and **Miguel A. Piery** for the Spanish translations

Ted Phillips, Sarah Vogwill, and **Edie Evans** for their help in page layout

Jana Collins for creating computer illustrations *and* page layouts

Lora Winslow for computer illustrations

Deborah Trella, Roy Mendl, and **Doug Prinzivalli** at Trella-Mendl Design Group Inc. for the Giant Step Press logo

Richardine and Larry Imrie for their personal and financial support

Special thanks to over 150 teachers and thousands of middle school and high school students that have experienced this unit and provided us with invaluable feedback.

Tim Scheidt & Jim Fina

TABLE OF CONTENTS

◆ ◆ ◆

FANTASY BASEBALL
Unit Overview

Two outs in the bottom of the ninth. Cecil Fielder of the American League Champion Detroit Tigers strolls to the plate. The record capacity crowd begins chanting, "Cecil, Cecil, Cecil" as the runners take their lead. It's Game 7 of the World Series. The Tigers are down by three. Cecil steps to the plate, glances at the runners at all three bases, then gives his patented icy cold stare to the opposing pitcher on the mound. Lee Smith of the St. Louis Cardinals stares back, glances over at the runner Trammell on third, then releases a blazing fastball headed directly toward the heart of the plate. The crowd roars at the crack of the bat — it's a long fly ball, hit deep to center field, way back, way back — it's, it's gone! A grand slam home run for Cecil Fielder! The Tigers win the series! The Tigers win the series!

Welcome to Fantasy Baseball — an integrated mathematics unit for the middle grades. This is a 5–8 week unit that blends the instruction and application of key mathematical concepts with an exciting, engaging real world context. During this unit, students become managers of their very own major league baseball team. They learn to analyze key statistical data, draft players, make trades, arrange lineups, play simulated games, etc., everything a major league manager has to do. With some strategic planning and a little luck, they might even lead their team to the Fantasy Baseball World Series.

Students use baseball cards to gather statistical data about major league baseball players. They learn to analyze the data in order to determine a players' offensive strengths and weaknesses. They then become co-managers of their own team, drafting and trading players to compile a final major league roster. A more detailed analysis is done of their players which leads to the creation of player wheels, proportionately accurate representations of a player's offensive statistics for a given year. These wheels are then used to play simulated games against other teams in the class. Statistics are consistently gathered, analyzed, compared and displayed by the students. A regular season schedule is created and carried out by the teams in the class. An optional League Championship Series and World Series is played to determine a class Fantasy Baseball champion.

This unit reflects the changes called for by national groups regarding the way mathematics is to be taught in our schools. It combines key mathematical content with an engaging context that provides students with the opportunity to solve problems, use reasoning skills and communicate mathematically. The following paragraphs describe some of the key features of this unit that address the concerns raised by these national groups.

Mathematical Content

This unit interweaves all mathematical strands outlined in the California Mathematics Framework and NCTM Curriculum and Evaluation Standards. Special attention is given to multiple representations, proportional reasoning, statistical analysis and probability. Throughout this unit, the students are expected to problem solve, develop and use reasoning skills and communicate mathematically.

Access & Equity

The mathematics presented in this unit is easily accessible to *all students,* from Chapter I to GATE. The unit allows for and fosters a range of abilities and mathematical understandings. The baseball context in which the unit appears crosses any ethnic and/or gender barriers that may exist in other contexts. Baseball (some form of the game) is played in countries all over the world by males and females alike. Many girls, often deprived of experiences similar to ones presented in this unit, find this an interesting way to learn and apply mathematics.

Cooperative Learning

Although this unit does not promote one researched method of cooperative learning, it is presented in such a way that students must work cooperatively. Co-managers, forced to make important decisions regarding their team, must work as a team. Throughout the unit, I have provided many resource guides, so students can't fall back on asking questions of you, the teacher. If they do, you can always refer them back to the resources they have available. In this way, you can also encourage them to take responsibility for their own learning, to work together and assist each other when possible. In the process, they learn to make use of one of their most valuable resources — their classmates.

Technology

This unit supports the view that students should not be expected to be human calculators but rather should learn to make use of the technology available to them. Because of the mathematical content explored in this unit, a fraction calculator is preferred for all students. If this is not possible, a four function calculator will suffice. The use of a computer spreadsheet is included in the unit as an optional activity. If computers and the appropriate software are available, this application is highly recommended.

Manager's Log

Following each activity in the unit, students are asked to respond in writing to a Manager's Log prompt. This supports the notion that students should be expected to communicate their mathematical reasoning, in writing, on a regular basis. These entries are to be used as assessment tools by the teacher as well as used to measure growth in the development of mathematical understanding.

Challenge Problems

Three Challenge Problems are integrated into the unit. These problems will involve some time to complete. Each problem is written using the baseball theme and applies an assortment of mathematical concepts. A worthwhile activity would be to have students work with their partner on a problem, then develop a class rubric specific to the problem and have the class score the papers. By doing this, students will have the chance to see a variety of approaches to the same problem and will learn to assess different levels of understanding.

I typically like to assign the Challenge Problems as P.O.W.'s (Problems of the Week)and give my students exactly one week to complete them. I hand the problem out on a Wednesday and spend about 10–15 minutes facilitating a discussion regarding ways my students might approach the problem. I then spend about 5–10 minutes on Friday, checking where they're at and another 5–10 minutes the following Tuesday doing the same. On the following Wednesday, we spend close to the whole period sharing our results, looking at the different approaches people had towards the same problem.

Assessment

Assessment is integrated throughout the unit, focusing on the work that students do. Students complete a pre-assessment at the start of the unit to be used for finding out what knowledge and experiences they bring into the unit. This is also used for comparison at the conclusion of the unit to measure growth in mathematical understanding.

Each task that the students complete can be assessed by using the Manager's Log responses. Quite often, the best assessment is the end product of each assigned task. Because each activity builds on the previous ones, students must have an understanding of what they are doing to proceed. Additional performance assessments are included for optional use at the end of approximately every other activity.

Two assessment pieces are provided at the end of the unit — an in-class individual assessment and a combined in class/out of class pair assessment. The individual assessment is closely aligned with the pre-assessment while the pair assessment (advertising display and presentation) allows for students to be creative and show off what they have learned. Both assessment pieces provide valuable information with regards to the students' levels of mathematical understanding.

Homework

There are no specific tasks that are designated purely as homework assignments. Many times the students will need additional time to complete a task and therefore can have it assigned as homework. The three Challenge Problems can also be assigned as homework if desired. Whether or not you ask your students to do homework, you may want to involve your students' parents in the new unit they are working on. On the next page, I have provided a Parent Letter that you can modify or reproduce to acquaint parents with Fantasy Baseball.

FANTASY BASEBALL
An Integrated Mathematics Unit

Dear Parents,

Your son/daughter is about to begin an exciting new math unit titled *Fantasy Baseball.* This unit reflects the changes called for by national groups regarding the way mathematics is taught in our schools. It combines key mathematical content with an engaging context that provides students with regular opportunities to solve problems, develop and use reasoning skills, and communicate mathematically.

A few of the important mathematical ideas that your son/daughter will be exploring are:

- **finding and using ratios to interpret data**
- **understanding and applying fraction/decimal/percentage equivalence**
- **collecting, organizing, displaying, analyzing and interpreting data**
- **constructing circle graphs proportionate to statistics on the backs of baseball cards**
- **differentiating between theoretical and experimental probability**

This unit is roughly 5–8 weeks long. The time may be extended depending on the interest and motivation of the students to explore parts of the unit in greater depth. Students will be expected to work in the manner mathematical work is done outside of school. This includes: solving non-routine problems; working in a collaborative manner with fellow students; producing quality work; communicating about mathematics both orally and in writing; using calculators and computers to solve problems; researching information; demonstrating initiative, creativity and persistence.

Students will be assessed in terms of the quality of work completed. The final assessment piece, a project/presentation that applies everything that has been learned, will require time outside of class as well as time in class. Students will be working with a partner and expected to complete the majority of this assignment outside of class.

As parents, you may help by encouraging your son or daughter. Provide support by asking him/her what he/she is working on in math class. Share your thoughts with your son or daughter regarding the work they are doing. You may help your student with the mathematics if you feel comfortable doing so but please be sure he/she understands any special techniques you use.

Respectfully,

Before You Begin . . .

I'm glad that you have decided to make Fantasy Baseball a part of your classroom experience. What follows is the most exciting unit I've ever taught and one that is packed with unlimited possibilities for exploring important mathematical concepts. In fact, this unit is so rich in the mathematics and captivates student interest to such a high degree that many teachers have extended the unit beyond the suggested time frame. I encourage you to run with this — use it as a roadmap but venture off into new investigations that interest you and your students as you proceed through the unit. No piece of curriculum fits perfectly (as is) in every classroom — mold this to meet your needs, to make it yours.

This unit is easily adapted to many different teaching situations. The last time I taught it, I started about three weeks into the school year (after class enrollment had stabilized and classroom procedures had been established). It took us a little over 5 weeks to reach Opening Day of the regular season. At this point, I had regular season games scheduled two days per week and spent the other days on new material. This worked great because it maintained student interest and I was also able to make important mathematical connections using contexts other than baseball. We wrapped our season just prior to Winter Break and completed the assessment pieces in early January.

Another time, I started the unit in March to coincide with spring training. We went straight through the unit and ended our regular season around the middle of May. The last few weeks of school were spent working on and presenting the pair projects along with the League Playoffs and World Series. This time frame also worked out well because with baseball season in full stride, interest and motivation remained high through the end of the year.

I have talked with a number of teachers that have used this unit at times other than the two I've mentioned. Some have taught the unit as a 9 week elective or explorative class, while still others have used it for intersession (year round schools) or summer school. To date, feedback from the teachers using the unit has been extremely positive, regardless of when it has been taught. You will need to take a look at your situation and decide the best method for presenting the unit to your students.

I know (through experience) that you and your students are headed towards some exciting times as you begin this unit. Have a great time and let me know about your successes.

Tim Scheidt

◆ ◆ ◆

PLEASE BE AWARE . . .
You will need to have baseball cards for your students to progress with this unit once you finish with the *Unit Preview*. Please turn to *Pre-Activity Preparation* in *Activity 1* at this time for information regarding the baseball cards you will need. Preparing now will avoid any future delays in proceeding with the unit.

DEDICATION

To my brother, Mike Scheidt, who long ago taught me that gathering, calculating and analyzing baseball statistics can be a great deal of fun. I'll never forget the countless number of "fantasy" games we played as kids with our prized collections of baseball cards. By the way Mike, have you seen my Joe Morgan recently?

FANTASY BASEBALL

An Integrated Mathematics Unit for the Middle Grades

Unit Preview

◆ ◆ ◆

Summary

Students write about their experiences, knowledge, and feelings about the game of baseball. They also complete a pre-assessment problem where they're asked to analyze the statistics of two ball players. The teacher can then read or have the students read *The Baseball Scoop* by Dan Greenberg, a short story that can be used to introduce baseball to those who are unfamiliar with it. Following a brief overview of the Fantasy Baseball unit, each student then selects a partner to co-manage a team. Co-managers then participate in a lottery to determine team names.

Math Content

- analysis of baseball statistics
- predicting the probability of an event

Classroom Time

2–3 days

Materials

Student Pages:

  Pre-Assessment — New Kids in Town (1 per student)

Transparencies:

  Major League Baseball Teams list

Paper and pencils

The Baseball Scoop by Dan Greenberg

Large chart paper (1 sheet)

2 sets of poker chips numbered 1–20

10" by 13" clasped envelopes (1 per team)

Colored pencils/markers/crayons

Pre-Activity Preparation

- Post a large sheet of chart paper at the front of the room and prepare it as shown below. Be sure to leave enough space to record 4–5 team names under each division.

	Major League Baseball	
	AMERICAN LEAGUE	
East	Central	West
	NATIONAL LEAGUE	
East	Central	West

- You will also want to prepare your two sets of chips numbered 1–20 and place each set in a separate container.

Getting Started — Students Write About Baseball

Tell your class that they are about to begin a unit that is centered around America's national pastime — baseball. You may want to share an anecdote or two about your experiences or knowledge of the game to capture students' attention. (I always like to share how I once stole second base with the bases loaded!) These experiences can be about baseball or softball — the key is to begin generating some pre-writing discussion about the sport.

After this short discussion, explain that you would like the students to do a short piece of writing for you. Tell them that this writing will strictly be used by you to get some sense of their experiences, knowledge or feelings about the game of baseball. Write the following two prompts on your chalkboard:

What I know about baseball . . .
How I feel about baseball and why . . .

Ask your students to select one of the two prompts to write on for 5–7 minutes. Encourage them to write as much as they can during this time. This writing is to be done individually without discussion so that students can express their personal thoughts and feelings about the game. Your students' writings will indicate which students have a high interest and/or knowledge of the game and which have low interest/knowledge.

Once the students have completed their writing, have them share what they have written with other members of their group. By first sharing in small groups, *every* student has the opportunity to read their writing to a captive audience. If you have students that would like to share with the whole class, you may want to allow a little extra time for this to occur. Once you feel that students have had ample opportunity to share their writing, collect their papers for your review.

Student Page

Name ______________
Date ______________
Period ______

FANTASY BASEBALL

Pre-Assessment — New Kids In Town

Imagine that two new kids have just moved into your neighborhood and are looking to play on a local baseball or softball team. You have been told by your coach that one of these students will be joining your team. Below are the statistics that they accumulated for their previous teams. Analyze these statistics to help you determine which player you would like to have on your team. On a separate sheet of paper, explain who you would select. Be sure to support your selection with the statistics that are given.

PLAYER A

AB	H	2B	3B	HR	BB	SO
37	13	4	0	5	3	9

PLAYER B

AB	H	2B	3B	HR	BB	SO
61	24	8	3	2	9	7

Which player would you select for your team — Player A? Player B? Explain your reasoning for the player you'd select.

Page 88 (Spanish page 130)

Pre-Assessment — New Kids In Town

As your students progress through this unit, they will learn to critically analyze players' statistics and calculate the probability of their players getting hits in clutch situations. These skills will help them to decide what players they want on their teams and how to place them in the batting order. In order to be able to measure their growth in this capacity, it is important to gather some baseline data about each student before they get too far into the unit. For this reason, I ask students to spend no more than 10 minutes responding to a pre-assessment problem.

In the pre-assessment problem, students analyze two players' statistics and make a decision about which one they would choose to have on their team. Assure your students that there is no "wrong answer" and that what's important is the reasoning they use to support their decision. Be sure to tell your students that this problem will not be graded but rather will be used as a tool to measure their growth as they proceed through the unit.

Pass out a copy of the pre-assessment problem (**Pre-Assessment — New Kids in Town**) to each student. Ask them to respond in writing on a separate sheet of paper that will be stapled to the problem sheet. Stress the importance of having them work on their own, without discussion, as you want to gather data on each individual. Explain to them that because this is a pre-assessment and you want to find out what they know, you will not be able to answer any questions they have about the problem.

Teacher Notes

Expect some of your students to have absolutely no clue as to how to approach this problem. Many of them may not know what some of the baseball abbreviations stand for. I suggest that you don't tell them at this time but let them struggle a little bit. I've had times where students selected "Player B" because their first name starts with a "B". I love these types of responses because I know that by the end of the unit, their answers to a similar problem will look entirely different. They always seem to get a kick out of comparing their responses to ones done at the conclusion of the unit.

***The Baseball Scoop:* A Baseball Resource**

Provided with this unit is a short piece of fiction titled *The Baseball Scoop* by Dan Greenberg. This story was written to help you and your students gain additional insight into the game of baseball and become familiar with some of the terminology before getting too far into the unit. You will find that taking some time to let your students experience this story will increase their comfort level about the game of baseball.

There are several different ways you can use this resource to get the maximum benefit from it. After reading the story yourself, you may want to read it aloud to your students, listing the key baseball terms and abbreviations that arise in context. You can then have your students work in small groups to discuss, research and share knowledge they possess or information they find about these terms. This is a great time to let the "baseball experts" in your class (and you will have some), serve as class resources. Having an open discussion and possibly simulating some of the terms can be of great benefit.

If you were able to purchase some additional copies of *The Baseball Scoop*, you may want to have your students do some partner reading/discussion or possibly use it like a play script with students taking on the roles of the different characters in the story. Once again, the purpose of this piece is to get you and all of your students to a level of comfort that will be of benefit as you progress through the unit. One other purpose is to provide a literature/language arts link to the mathematics in the unit. Throughout the unit, your students will be asked to communicate their feelings, thinking and reasoning in written form. You may want to take a look at the Manager's Log at the end of Activity 8 where it suggests that students be involved in writing a Fantasy Baseball newsletter. Let your students know that they too will have the opportunity to be reporters like Matt and Rickie when they get into their Fantasy Baseball regular season.

Providing a Unit Overview

Your students will be very curious to know what this unit is all about. Some will be excited while others will be somewhat apprehensive. I suggest at this time that you give the students a brief 5–10 minute overview of the unit. You might consider reading them the first page of the **Unit Overview** on page vii. If you have attended the two-day training or have taught the unit before, you may want to share some of your own experiences and/or feelings about the unit. The mind-set that you provide is crucial to the success of this unit. Be sure to acknowledge that the students are all coming into the unit with different experiences, knowledge and abilities. Explain to them that the beauty of this unit is that each of them will be able to successfully increase their knowledge of baseball and math while having a great deal of fun along the way.

Teacher Notes

Having the students work in pairs serves a variety of purposes. It encourages the managers to communicate and share the work; it also allows you to progress through the unit even during student absences. It is rare that both managers are absent on the same day so one usually holds down the fort for the other. This way the class can maintain the somewhat hectic pace that occurs during the "regular season."

Selecting Co-Managers/Team Lottery

I have found that the best way to implement this unit is by having students work in pairs as co-managers of a Fantasy Baseball team. I allow the students to pair up on their own. I want them to feel as comfortable as possible with the person they'll be spending a great deal of time with. In some cases, due to an odd number in your class, a student will have to work alone. It is not an impossible task but I strongly recommend that if you must have a student work alone that this student possess a high interest in math and baseball and be self-motivated. Another option, which I have used successfully several times, is for you, yourself, to become a co-manager, with the understanding that the student will end up carrying most of the load.

Transparency Master

MAJOR LEAGUE BASEBALL TEAMS

NATIONAL LEAGUE

EAST	CENTRAL	WEST
Atlanta Braves	Chicago Cubs	Colorado Rockies
Florida Marlins	Cincinnati Reds	Los Angeles Dodgers
Montreal Expos	Houston Astros	San Diego Padres
New York Mets	Pittsburgh Pirates	San Francisco Giants
Philadelphia Phillies	St. Louis Cardinals	

AMERICAN LEAGUE

EAST	CENTRAL	WEST
Baltimore Orioles	Chicago White Sox	California Angels
Boston Red Sox	Cleveland Indians	Oakland Athletics
Detroit Tigers	Kansas City Royals	Seattle Mariners
New York Yankees	Milwaukee Brewers	Texas Rangers
Toronto Blue Jays	Minnesota Twins	

Page 89 (Spanish page 131)

Engage the students in a brainstorming session to generate a list of the Major League baseball teams. As students recall different teams, write the names on the chart that you posted at the front of the room. You can refer to the **Major League Baseball Teams** guide in order to place teams in the proper league and division.

Once you have listed all 28 teams, have the students participate in a lottery to determine which team they will manage for their Fantasy Baseball season. You will need your two sets of poker chips numbered 1–20. Count the number of teams you have in your class and leave that number of chips in each container (e.g. if you have 16 teams, chips #1–#16 remain in each container). Select one of the containers and pass out a chip to each pair of students.

Tell your students that you will be drawing chips from the other container to determine the order of team selection. I use this process so that the pair of students that receive chip #16 and initially think they get the last selection, come to life when they realize they can actually get the first pick in the lottery selection.

Prior to drawing numbers and having the students select their teams, have them write down the three team names they would most like to manage, in order of their preference. Ask your students to keep the names to themselves. This will prevent some students from selecting a team just so that another pair can't manage it. Also, explain to your students that they should strictly be selecting a team name without reference to the players that actually play for that team. In Fantasy Baseball, they will be receiving and trading players from all the teams in the league, not just the team whose name they pick.

After students have written down their three teams in order of preference, ask them:

How many of you think you have a good chance of getting your first team of choice?

Whether they think they have a good chance or not, ask them to give their reasoning for their prediction. Draw the following chart on the chalkboard to record their predictions and actual results:

TEAM CHOICE	ESTIMATE	ACTUAL
1st		
2nd		
3rd		
Other		

Ask for a show of hands to respond to the following questions:

How many of you think you will get your first choice of the three teams you wrote down? How many of you think you will get your second choice? third choice? How many think you will have to choose another team other than the three you have written down?

Allow your students to informally discuss their responses to these questions. Consider the following for a class with 30 students (15 teams): Mathematically all but one pair has a 50% or better chance of getting their first team of choice; because there are 28 Major League teams to choose from, the first pair of students has a 28/28 chance of picking their team, the second pair has a 27/28 chance, and so on with the last pair having a 13/28 chance. But there are other factors that need to be taken into account. For example, when calculating the mathematical possibilities, each Major League team is considered equally desirable to another; but in the classroom, there tends to be a select number of popular teams. Many students often want the same team names, so the theoretical probabilities and experimental probabilities may differ markedly when you run the team lottery in your classroom.

Teacher Notes

This is a good opportunity to get students thinking about probability without launching into a thorough investigation just yet. Here they can begin to look at mathematical possibilities as well as consider other variables that can affect the probability of certain outcomes. What's important for your students to grasp is that a probabilistic event will not necessarily yield the same results if duplicated.

After this brief discussion, proceed with the team lottery. As each pair of students selects their team of choice, draw a line through the team on the master chart to designate that it has been selected. After running the team lottery, ask the students whether or not they received their first team of choice, second team, third team or had to select an alternative team. Record these results on the chart so the students can compare them with their estimates.

When the lottery is finished, have your students calculate the percentage of students that received their first choice of teams, second choice, third choice and alternate. Then give them the following questions to think about:

> ***Were you surprised by the results of our team lottery? If so, what did you find surprising about the results?***
>
> ***Do you think these results would look any different if we were to hold the lottery again? Why or why not?***

Allow a few minutes for students to share their responses to these questions along with their reasoning. You may want to run a mock lottery to compare the results to your students' responses.

Preview Wrap — Team Envelope

Pass out one 10" by 13" clasp envelope to each of your new Fantasy Baseball teams. Tell the co-managers that this envelope will be used for keeping many of the papers/tools that they will receive or create during the unit. Explain that it will be extremely important for students to hold on to everything they receive and do since the final activity of the unit allows them to use any available materials that they gather from participating in the unit.

Assign your students the job of designing their team envelope using the team's traditional logo or an original if they'd like to create one. They should also put their names on the outside of the envelope. Tell your students that the designed envelopes will be kept in the classroom so that they can have easy access to them each day. I use a letter/legal size storage box for each classroom set of envelopes. Although the box seems quite empty with just the envelopes, it fills up rather quickly as students accumulate resources I provide and tools they create. By collecting the team envelopes each day, I avoid any problems in the event that a team's co-manager is absent from class.

Teacher Notes

You may want to consider bringing in pictures of each team's logo for students to refer to. These can be found in books, sets of stickers, pennants, etc. These items are usually found in your local sporting goods store. Some students get hung up on designing their team envelope because they want to reproduce the actual team logo. By having this available as a resource, you may avoid having students get frustrated and shutting down during this task.

Looking Ahead

Inform your students that over the next couple of days they will be looking at baseball cards and learning to make some sense of the statistics on the backs of the cards. Encourage them to talk with friends and family members to get any ideas about what might be key characteristics to look for. Assure those students feeling that they are at a disadvantage, that they will learn how to evaluate players so that they'll be able to compile as strong a baseball team as anyone else.

Activity 1
Making Sense of Player Statistics

◆ ◆ ◆

Summary

Students look at player statistics on the backs of baseball cards. They learn to calculate certain ratios and averages to determine below average, average and excellent offensive statistics. Each team receives their initial draft of players, distributed randomly. Managers construct a statistical comparison chart to aid them during the upcoming trade and free agent draft session.

Math Content

- calculating statistical averages and percentages
- determining unit ratios
- solving proportion problems
- multiple representations of data
- analysis of baseball statistics

Classroom Time

3–4 days

Materials

Student Pages:

Baseball Card Glossary (1 per student)
Player Guidelines (1 per student)
Player Comparison Chart (2 per team)

Transparencies:

Robin Ventura Card
Player Comparison Chart
Activity 1 Manager's Log
Activity 1 Performance Assessment

Baseball cards (1 box — 36 ct. packages)
Paper and pencils
Calculators (1 per student)
Manager's Log (journal) 1 per student

Pre-Activity Preparation

There are different ways of preparing for this activity, depending on how you choose to distribute the player cards to your students. First, select one of the options and follow the suggestions for activity preparation:

1. If you are using a box of 36 individual packets, open enough packets so that you have enough eligible players for every student in your class to receive one card. An eligible player is one that plays a position other than pitcher, has played for a Major League team recently, and has

logged at least 200 at bats (AB) during any one year of his Major League career. Players that do not have at least one year with 200 or more at bats are considered ineligible. This is because their statistics (based on less than 200 at bats) do not accurately reflect what they would do over the course of a whole season. Draft picks and players with only Minor League experience are also considered ineligible. For a class of 30 students you will probably need to open 4 or 5 packages. Set aside a package for each team (pair of students) in your class. The remaining cards will be used for the free agent draft.

2. If you are using a factory set containing somewhere around 800 cards, you will want to allow yourself enough time to sort through the cards prior to this activity. You may want to sort the cards into one of two ways:

   A. **By Team** — you can sort the cards into their actual teams. When it is time to give the cards to the managers, they can sort through the cards to determine the eligible players.

   B. **By Position** — you can sort the cards according to the position(s) the player plays. If you choose this method, you will need to weed out the pitchers, draft picks, minor league players, etc. For those players that can play two positions (for example, 2B - SS), placing them at either position will do.

You will find that if you are using a factory set, you will have a great deal of cards in excess that cannot be used for Fantasy Baseball. On the other hand, a factory set may yield enough cards for you to furnish two classes with the cards necessary to participate in the unit. It really comes down to personal choice and card availability.

Teacher Notes

I personally recommend using the box of individually wrapped packages with your students. There is a level of excitement that can't be matched when you pass out the packages and the students rip them open to see the players they might keep for their teams.

Understanding Player Statistics

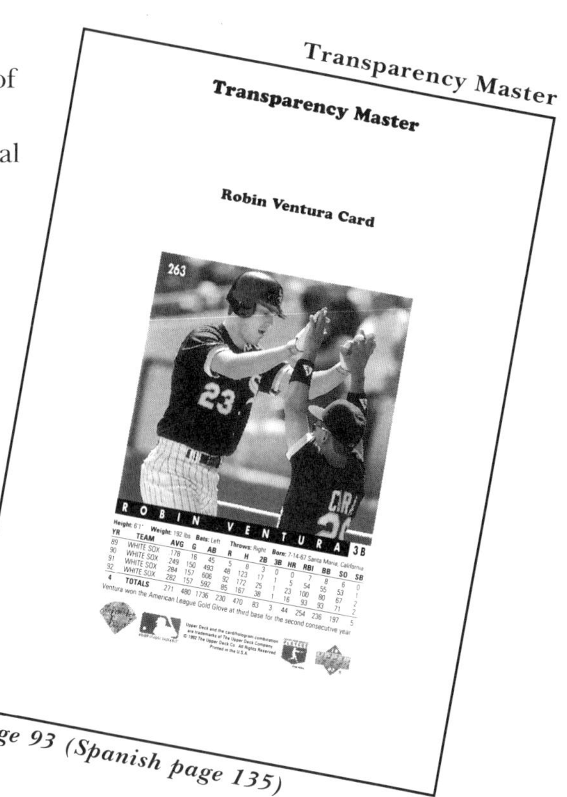

As previously mentioned, your students will enter this unit with a wide range of interest, knowledge and experience with respect to the game of baseball. Explain that the purpose of this activity is to give all of them some fundamental knowledge of baseball statistics so that they'll be able to make educated decisions when it comes time to put together their Fantasy Baseball teams. Tell them that by the time they're done, they will be able to easily distinguish between players that possess below average statistics, average statistics and excellent statistics. This knowledge will enable them to put together a strong, competitive team.

Pass out 1 card (eligible player) to each student in the class. You will hear some oohs and aahs as students recognize the names of popular players. Tell your students that they are to hold on to the card they receive and are not allowed to make trades at this time. Explain that there will be a time for trading cards after everyone has some common knowledge of player statistics. Have them look at the backs of their cards as you go over the meaning of each statistical category. You can use the **Robin Ventura Card** transparency as an example you can share with your class as you engage in this discussion. (This is a facsimile of an actual baseball card. The statistics from this card will be referred to throughout this unit.) This is also a good opportunity to let those students who are knowledgeable "show their stuff" and become the "class experts".

Have your students look at the statistics under the picture on the card. Tell them that for now, they will need to focus on the player's last year of service with a Major League team in which they had 200+ AB's, not their Major League totals. Proceed to go through each statistical category, giving a brief description of what it means or soliciting a description from one of your "class experts". At this point, you will also want to pass out a copy of the **Baseball Card Glossary** for your students to refer to and keep as a resource.

Teacher Notes

I like to place bases in the classroom at this time and have the students simulate as many of the statistics as possible. For example, by placing bases in the classroom and having a student represent a runner on third base, I can simulate an RBI (run batted in) by having the next batter get a single. This is effective for helping students gain a better understanding of where some of these statistics come from. It also allows my "experts" to share their knowledge with the class and gives the "newcomers" to the game, an opportunity to visualize most of the statistics.

Why Look At Statistics?

What do these statistics on the backs of baseball cards really mean? Why should we look at them? These are questions that your students may ask or you may want to ask them. Ask for two volunteers to read you the statistics for their players (without revealing their names) for any eligible year (Major League team - 200+ AB's). Record these statistics on the chalkboard or overhead using a chart similar to the one below.

PLAYER	AB	R	H	2B	3B	HR	RBI	SB	BB	SO
#1										
#2										

Student Page

BASEBALL CARD GLOSSARY

YR — the **year** the player played for a given team.

TEAM — the **team** played for during the year. Major League teams are represented by the team name **(Tigers, Giants, etc.)**. Minor League teams are represented by the city in which the team resides **(Nashville, Eugene, etc.)**

AVG — this number represents the player's **batting average**. This average is the decimal equivalent of the ratio of hits to official at bats.

G — the number of **games** the player appeared in for the team.

AB — this represents the number of **official at bats** the player had during the season. Official at bats (AB) do not include walks (BB) or sacrifice hits (bunts, sacrifice flies). Sacrifice hits do not count as at bats because the player makes an expected out in order to advance the runner(s).

R — the number of **runs** the player scored (times he crossed home plate).

H — the number of **hits** a player got during the season. This number represents the total singles, doubles, triples and home runs the player accumulated during the season.

2B — the number of **doubles** or times the player reached second base safely due to a hit.

3B — the number of **triples** or times the player reached third base safely due to a hit.

HR — the number of **home runs** the player hit during the season.

RBI — the number of **runs batted in** that the player was credited with during the season. This means that other players scored runs due to the player's hitting performance.

BB — the number of **walks** (also known as **bases on balls**) the player received during the season.

SO — the number of **strikeouts** the player had during the season.

SB — the number of **stolen bases** the player had during the season.

Page 90 (Spanish page 132)

Ask your students:

According to these statistics, which player is better? How do you know?

Allow your students a few minutes to respond to these questions, encouraging them to listen closely to each other's reasoning. After this discussion, ask:

Which player gets a hit most often? Which player gets on base most often? How do you know?

Once again, allow students to discuss their responses to these questions. Quite possibly you will find that the terms *batting average* and *on-base percentage* come up in this discussion. This is a good opportunity to calculate (or better yet, have students calculate) the batting average and on-base percentage for each of the players. (See Calculating Key Statistics on pp. 15–16 for instructions.) Once these statistics have been calculated, discuss the benefits of having some sort of baseline to compare players. Let your students know that these are two key statistics that they will initially use to compare players as they begin to establish their own Fantasy Baseball teams.

Tell your students that along with the afore-mentioned statistics, they will be using some additional measures to compare players. Explain that to fully understand their importance, they will be taking a brief excursion away from the context of baseball.

Teacher Notes

After I record the statistics for the first player, I ask for a second player that has around 200 fewer or 200 more at bats than the first player. My purpose for doing this is to have statistics that are not easy to compare without performing some calculations. My eventual goal is for my students to see that the purpose for using decimals and percentages in baseball statistics is to provide a baseline for comparison.

What Is a Ratio?

What is a ratio? How can ratios be useful to us?

Have your students discuss these questions in small, cooperative groups. If the concept of a ratio is review for your students, you may want to briefly touch on some of the following exercises, then proceed with the baseball context. If the concept of ratio is new to your students, a longer period of time will need to be spent developing this concept. The following can be used as a means to spark some discussion about ratios and their purpose.

Present your students with the following definition and example:

A ratio is a pair of positive numbers that is used to compare two sets. ***For example, the ratio of boys to girls in one of my 7th grade classes was 3 to 4. This means that for every three boys in my class, there were four girls. Point out that there are two common notations for ratios. The ratio of boys to girls in my class can be written as 3:4 or 3/4 and is read as "3 to 4."***

You may want to have them discuss how many boys and girls they think there were in the class presented in the example. Then in small groups, or as a whole class, have your students find and record ratios (using both notations) for any or all of the following:

- number of boys to girls in the class
- number of right handed students to left handed students
- number of tie shoes to slip-ons
- number of only children to number with siblings
- number of those that can roll their tongues to number that can't
- number of those with attached ear lobes to number of those with detached ear lobes
- number of those with freckles to number without
- other ratios that may be of interest to your students

Once you are confident that your students have a firm understanding of ratios, ask them to consider how ratios might be useful for looking at baseball statistics. Explain that they will be using what they have learned about ratios to calculate some additional statistics that will aid them in selecting productive players for their Fantasy Baseball teams.

Teacher Notes

I find it useful to venture away from the baseball context for a short while, regardless of whether the concept of ratio is new or review. It's nice for the students to see how a mathematical concept can be applied in several different contexts. It also gives students that aren't yet comfortable with the baseball context, an opportunity to experience something other than baseball. I usually find however, that most students are anxious to return to the baseball context and apply what they have learned.

Back to Baseball — Finding Unit Ratios

Ask your students:

> ***What is a team's objective when playing a game of baseball? What are they trying to accomplish?***

You will get responses from "scoring runs" to "winning games" to "crushing the other team!" The discussion should yield the fact that games are won by scoring more runs than the other team. Once this is clear, present students with some additional questions:

> ***What is the most important statistic for scoring runs recorded on the backs of baseball cards? Explain your reasoning.***
>
> ***What is the least important statistic for scoring runs recorded on the backs of baseball cards? Explain your reasoning.***

Allow some time for students to discuss these questions. Note that in major league baseball, a team's ability both to score runs and to prevent the other team from scoring runs are crucial to success. (A game that is won by a score of 1–0 counts just as much as a game that is won by a score of 15–14!) For the purposes of Fantasy Baseball, however, it is more important to determine who are the players with good offensive statistics (who help the team score runs) than who are the players with good defensive statistics. Because of this, you should help students see that a home run is the most productive statistic because it scores a run for the team and also scores any other runners that might be on base. The least productive statistic is a strikeout because it not only records an out for the team, it does not advance any runners that might be on base.

Explain to your students that they are going to apply their knowledge of ratios with these two statistics to provide them with data that they will use as they begin to put together their teams.

Present your students with the following hypothetical data on the chalkboard or overhead. Ask them to look at the data and think about which of these two players they would select for their team if they were given the choice and why.

Name	AB	H	HR	BB	SO
R. Crowe	562	173	15	67	63
J. Fina	381	103	14	42	57

You may want to have your students calculate the batting average and on-base percentage for each player. This will provide them with some additional data for comparison; the question to keep asking them is if they have enough data to make a reasonable decision. Tell your students to look closely at the HR's and SO's for each player. Ask them if it is possible to compare these statistics to determine which player is better. Allow for some discussion, encouraging students to share their thinking with the class.

Most of your students will find it difficult to compare these two statistics. They may initially say that one has more HR's than the other or one has less SO's than the other but something will not feel right to them. Tell them that you want them to look at these statistics from a different angle.

Ask your students:

> ***How can we find out how often each of these players gets a home run? How can we find out how often each player records a strikeout?***

Remind the students that the number of BB's (bases on balls) are not included in the number of AB's and will need to be added to get the number of cumulative at bats for each player. This number of Cum. AB's should be used along with the number of HR's and SO's to answer these questions.

Your students will have a variety of methods for finding answers to these questions. Point out to them that when they are finding out how often a player is getting a HR or a SO, they are finding unit ratios. A unit ratio is a ratio that has been reduced so that the number 1 is representative of the first set. In other words, finding out how often R. Crowe gets a HR can be written as 1:37.352941 or rounded to 1:37. This means that he averages 1 HR for every 37 times he steps to the plate.

Allow your students to calculate, compare and discuss the results of finding unit ratios for these two players. This will provide good practice for them as later they will be asked to calculate these for the players they receive in their initial draft.

Explain to your students that given the time you have, it will be impossible to look critically at every facet of a player's game. Because of this time limitation, explain that they will be calculating and analyzing the four statistics they have been introduced to: batting average, on-base percentage, HR:Cum. AB ratio and SO:Cum. AB ratio. These measures will be useful in helping them to determine which players they will eventually keep for their Fantasy Baseball teams.

Calculating Key Statistics

Modeling how to calculate the four key statistics might serve as valuable reinforcement for your students when it comes time for them to do calculations for the players they will initially receive. If you elect to go through this process with the entire class, use the statistics from the 1991 season on the Robin Ventura card on page 93. Be sure to have your students discuss what each calculation represents and how it will be useful for deciding which players they may want to keep for their teams.

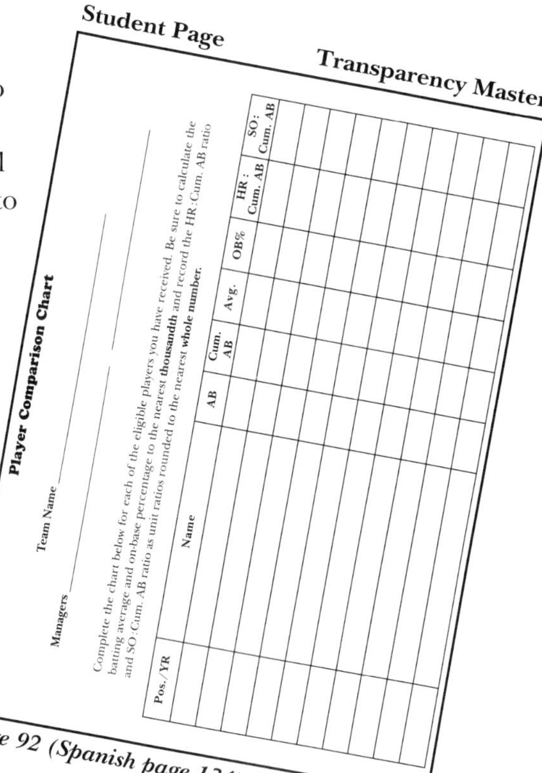

The following information is not intended to be duplicated and given to students but rather for you, the teacher, to use as a resource. This information will help you explain to your students what you are doing as you model calculating some key statistics from the Robin Ventura card. You may want to have your students take notes as you work through your example. A **Player Comparison Chart** is provided for duplication to use with your students. Your students may also want to record formulas or methods for calculating these statistics as they are not included on the **Player Comparison Charts.**

BATTING AVERAGE

Although players' batting averages are recorded on their cards, it will be helpful to show students how to calculate them. A player's batting average is found by dividing the number of hits (H) the player has by the number of official at bats (AB). The calculator display will often show more than three digits when performing this operation. Explain that the average is rounded to the thousandths place because this provides baseball analysts with the accuracy they need for most purposes (i.e. batting champions). On occasion, averages are carried out to four and five digits when the need arises. This figure represents the percentage of time a player reaches base via a hit (single, double, triple or home run).

ON-BASE PERCENTAGE

This statistic shows the percentage of time a player can be expected to reach base safely, via a hit or a walk. The language can be misleading as it is called a percentage, yet the statistic is represented as a decimal and carried out to the thousandths place (same as average). The higher the percentage, the more likely the player is to reach base safely. This percentage is found by dividing the number of times a player reached base safely (H + BB) by their total at bats (AB + BB). Using Robin's 1991 statistics, 172 hits (H) + 80 walks (BB) = 252 times he reached base safely. This figure of 252 divided by his total at bats (686) yields a figure of .3673469. This decimal, rounded off to the nearest thousandth, represents a .367 on-base percentage. This calculation means that during the 1991 season, Robin reached base safely (due to a hit or walk) around 37% of the time.

HR:CUM. AB RATIO

This measure shows, on the average, how often (# of AB's) a player can be expected to hit a home run. This ratio is calculated as a unit ratio (e.g. 1: __) in order to use for comparison with other players. This statistic is important because a player hitting a home run not only scores a run for the team, they hit in any other player that is on base prior to their hitting the home run. This means RBI's (runs batted in) for the hitter and runs scored for the team. To be as accurate as possible, you must first find the number of cumulative at bats a player had during the season. This is done by adding the official at bats (AB) and the walks (BB).

Using Robin Ventura's figures from the 1991 season, 606 AB's plus 80 BB's would equal 686 cumulative at bats. You can find his HR:Cum. AB ratio by dividing the number of total at bats (AB + BB) by the number of home runs (HR). Using Robin Ventura's statistics from the 1991 season, his 686 cumulative at bats divided by his 23 HR's yields a figure of 29.826087. To simplify this as a unit ratio, we round off to the nearest whole number. By doing this we find that Robin's HR:Cum. AB ratio is 1:30. In other words, during the 1991 season, Robin Ventura averaged a home run every 30 times he went to the plate.

SO:CUM. AB RATIO

This measure shows, on the average, how often (# of AB's) a player can be expected to strike out. This ratio is also calculated as a unit ratio to use for comparison purposes. This statistic is important because not only does a strikeout represent an out, runners on base can not advance when this occurs. This ratio is found by dividing the number of cumulative at bats (AB + BB) by the number of strikeouts (SO). Again, using Robin Ventura's statistics from the 1991 season, his 686 cumulative at bats divided by his 67 SO's yields a figure of 10.238806. Rounded to the nearest whole number, Robin's SO:Cum. AB ratio is 1:10. In other words, during the 1991 season, Robin Ventura struck out, on the average, once every 10 times he went to the plate.

What Makes a Player Worth Keeping?

How do I know if a player is any good? How do I know if I should keep a player or trade him?

These are questions that will arise after your experiences with finding the different percentages and ratios. Let your students know that they will arrive at some type of answer to these questions after a brief investigation of player statistics.

Instruct your students to calculate the four key statistics (batting avg., on-base %, HR:Cum. AB and SO:Cum. AB) for the player card in their possession. Once they have done this for their card, tell them to exchange cards with their co-manager and do the same for the new card. Once they have calculated the four statistics for both cards, have them compare their results with their co-manager.

Present the following to your students:

> ***Figuring out which player is best by looking at batting average or on-base % is fairly easy. It is obvious that the higher the average and/or percentage, the better the player. What about the ratios of HR : Cum. AB and SO : Cum. AB? What determines whether or not a ratio can be considered favorable or unfavorable?***

Allow your students a few minutes to discuss this in small groups, then as a whole class. Explain that you would like to have them solve some proportion problems to help them better understand the meaning and value of these ratios. Solving these proportion problems will help them to see the differences that would occur for players having different ratios and the same number of at bats. This will help to further their understanding of the impact of these ratios prior to establishing their own teams.

Write the following on the overhead or chalkboard:

HR:Cum. AB = 1:22

This ratio can also be represented as a fraction:

$$\frac{HR}{AB} = \frac{1}{22}$$

This means that on the average, this player gets 1 HR every 22 at bats.

> ***How many home runs would you expect this player to get if they were up to bat 100 times?***

Let your students play around with this question. As students come up with an answer, let them show their methods for arriving at one. You may see these two methods or others generated by the students:

- If this player gets 1 HR every 22 at bats then I'll divide 100 by 22 and get 4.5454545. By rounding up, I think this player will get 5 HR's in 100 at bats.

- Let's see, $\frac{1}{22} = \frac{2}{44} = \frac{3}{66} = \frac{4}{88} = \frac{5}{110}$. I think this player will get 4 HR's in 100 at bats because they would need 110 at bats to get 5 HR's.

Discuss the different methods that the students come up with to answer this question. Acknowledge the fact that they may come up with slightly different answers depending on the method they use.

Tell your students that you want them to think about the following questions:

Which is better, a unit ratio with a large number or a small number? Explain your answer.

Explain that you want them to use the ratios they calculated from their card to investigate a series of tasks. As they complete these tasks, the answer to the question above should become obvious to them. Write these tasks on the overhead or chalkboard:

- ***Using the unit ratios you calculated for your two players, find the approximate number of HR's and SO's you would expect your players to get in 200 AB's.***
- ***Using these same ratios, find the approximate numbers for 358 AB's.***
- ***Once again, find for 486 AB's.***
- ***Finally, find for 637 AB's.***

Student Page

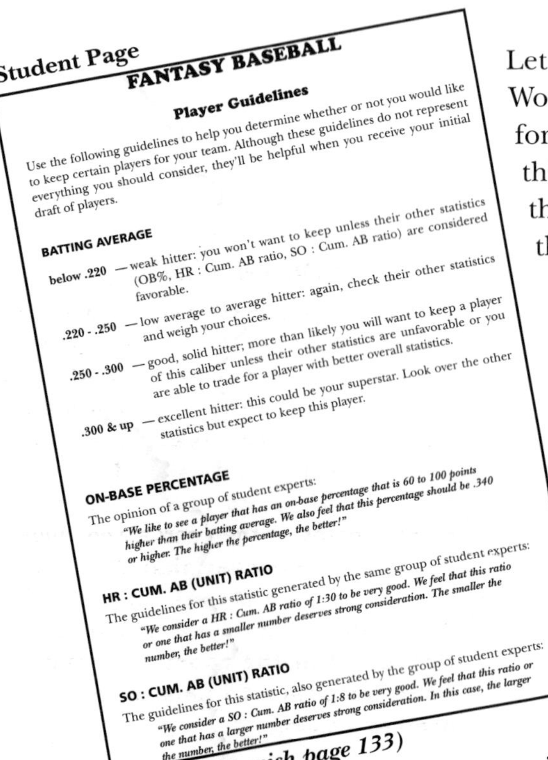

FANTASY BASEBALL

Player Guidelines

Use the following guidelines to help you determine whether or not you would like to keep certain players for your team. Although these guidelines do not represent everything you should consider, they'll be helpful when you receive your initial draft of players.

BATTING AVERAGE

below .220 — weak hitter: you won't want to keep unless their other statistics (OB%, HR : Cum. AB ratio, SO : Cum. AB ratio) are considered favorable.

.220 - .250 — low average to average hitter: again, check their other statistics and weigh your choices.

.250 - .300 — good, solid hitter; more than likely you will want to keep a player of this caliber unless their other statistics are unfavorable or you are able to trade for a player with better overall statistics.

.300 & up — excellent hitter: this could be your superstar. Look over the other statistics but expect to keep this player.

ON-BASE PERCENTAGE

The opinion of a group of student experts:

"We like to see a player that has an on-base percentage that is 60 to 100 points higher than their batting average. We also feel that this percentage should be .340 or higher. The higher the percentage, the better!"

HR : CUM. AB (UNIT) RATIO

The guidelines for this statistic generated by the same group of student experts:

"We consider a HR : Cum. AB ratio of 1:30 to be very good. We feel that this ratio or one that has a smaller number deserves strong consideration. The smaller the number, the better!"

SO : CUM. AB (UNIT) RATIO

The guidelines for this statistic, also generated by the group of student experts:

"We consider a SO : Cum. AB ratio of 1:8 to be very good. We feel that this ratio or one that has a larger number deserves strong consideration. In this case, the larger the number, the better!"

Page 91 (Spanish page 133)

Let your students complete this series of tasks, then compare their results. Working with "messy" numbers, they will need to be creative with their methods for approximating their answers. Precision is not of the utmost importance at this point. What is important is that your students begin to see that the larger the number in the unit ratio, the fewer HR's or SO's a player has. Conversely, the smaller the number in the unit ratio, the more HR's or SO's a player has.

Students can explore this further by trading cards and solving additional proportion problems. What's important is to get them to see that HR's are a productive statistic so it is best to have a player with a smaller number in the HR:Cum. AB (unit) Ratio. On the other hand, SO's are non-productive so it is best to have a player with a larger number in the SO:Cum. AB (unit) Ratio.

After students have had a chance to investigate the meaning of ratios, pass out copies of the **Player Guidelines**. These guidelines for determining whether or not a player would be worthwhile to keep were created by a group of "student experts" in my class. Have your students discuss the guidelines for each of the statistics and tell whether they agree or disagree with the student recommendations. You may wish to have them revise these guidelines or create their own based on the class discussion that develops. In any case, using some sort of criteria for "good" percentages and ratios will help your students as they proceed to formulate their teams for the Fantasy Baseball season.

Initial Player Draft/Calculating Their Worth

It is time to present your student managers with their initial draft of players. How you hold this draft will largely depend on which packaging selection of cards you decided on at the beginning of this activity. I suggest doing one of the following:

1. If you are using individual packages, present each team with a package of cards. They will need to sort out unusable cards and set them aside. Most packages will contain 6-9 usable baseball cards (players with at least 200 Major League AB's during one season). Combined with the two cards the teams received earlier, they will have at least 8 usable cards to begin with. Tell the students to set the pitcher's cards aside also as they will going back to them at a later time.

2. If you are using a factory set and **have** sorted the cards by team, you can present each managerial pair with their cards from their team. The cards that are not distributed can then be used in the free agent draft that is held later. Again, students will want to sort through the cards to select the usable ones.

3. If you are using a factory set but **have not** sorted them into teams, you can present each team with a random selection of 8–10 cards, assuming you have already sorted them into usable and unusable. Be sure to keep the pitchers close by as students will be selecting from them in the near future.

Let your students know that by the end of the initial draft, any trading and the free agent draft, they will need to have 10 cards of players that are considered eligible. In order to field a complete team, they will need to have the following on their roster:

catcher - 1
first baseman - 1
second baseman - 1
shortstop - 1
third baseman - 1
outfielders - 3
pitchers - 2

Let your students know that they will need to select 2 pitchers from the cards they have to place at the bottom of their final roster. Although they will only need one pitcher for a game, they are allowed two for the fun of alternating

Teacher Notes

This is an excellent time to form a baseball diamond in your classroom and have students stand in each of the nine positions. You may also want to have a discussion as to why it is important to have a player at each position. As your students begin looking at their cards, they will need to be reminded that they will eventually need players for each of the positions. I always post the position chart in the room to remind them from time to time what they need to acquire.

pitchers on game days. Let them know that they will learn the role of their pitchers in Fantasy Baseball in a future activity.

Teacher Notes

I take advantage of this time to go to each team and personally stress the importance of working together as a team. I also refer any questions they have to other students or get them to look back at the information sheets they've received. I want them to consistently use the resources available to them.

Once each team has received their initial draft of players, it is time for them to calculate the baseline data that will help the managers to decide which players they want to keep. Let your students know that to keep with the "fantasy" theme of Fantasy Baseball, they may use the statistics from any year that a player has 200+ AB's for a major league team. Let them know that the year they select can vary from player to player.

Pass out a copy of the **Player Comparison Chart** to each co-manager. Explain that they are to calculate the four statistics (batting avg., on-base %, HR:Cum. AB, SO:Cum. AB) for each eligible player to complete their team chart. Some students may end up with more than one player for some positions and no players for other positions. This is not uncommon and will be flushed out through the trading sessions and Free Agent Draft. At this time they should calculate the statistics for each eligible player as they will want this information for the trading sessions. You may want to point out that one of these statistics, batting average, is found on the card itself. Tell them that each co-manager should complete a copy to use for the upcoming trading session and Free Agent Draft. Point out that each team must complete two copies of this chart prior to being allowed to enter into trade talks with other teams.

Teacher Notes

On occasion I have decided not to use the *Player Comparison Charts* but rather have students construct their own charts. This depends on the amount of time I have and whether or not I feel it would be beneficial to have the students using self-constructed charts. This does provide an excellent opportunity for looking at the various ways that people collect and organize information.

Activity Wrap — Comparing Players

You can expect that each of your teams will finish in a different period of time. When you notice that a team is finished, encourage them to have another team do a spot check of their work. This spot check consists of selecting two players and calculating their statistics as a way of checking for accuracy. In most cases, errors will be readily apparent. For example, if a team has a player with a HR : Cum. AB ratio of 1:3, this would be the equivalent of getting one home run every 3 at bats, or 200 HR's in 600 AB's. Seeing as how the Major League record for home runs in a season is 61, this would be an unreasonable ratio. A reasonable ratio for a power hitter would be more like 1:20 which would equate to 30 HR's in 600 AB's. Insist that each team have another do a spot check on their statistics before being considered eligible for trade talks.

Encourage your students to start looking closely at the players' statistics and begin thinking about which players they definitely want to keep on their team. They may want to refer to the **Player Guidelines**. Point out that it is rare to get a player that looks great in all four categories and that what they'll most likely want on their team is a balanced attack. They'll want players that hit for average, players with power and players that get on base a high percentage of the time. Tell your students to highlight those players that they're pretty certain they will keep for their team.

Manager's Log (journal)

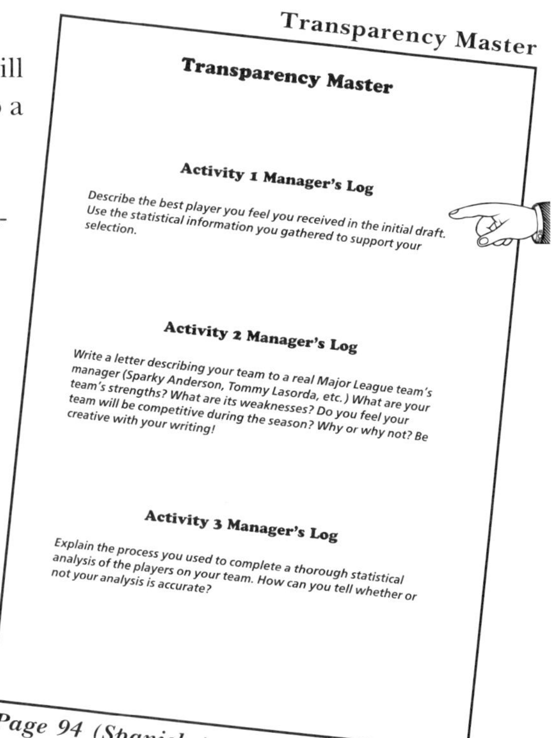
Transparency Master

Transparency Master

Activity 1 Manager's Log

Describe the best player you feel you received in the initial draft. Use the statistical information you gathered to support your selection.

Activity 2 Manager's Log

Write a letter describing your team to a real Major League team's manager (Sparky Anderson, Tommy Lasorda, etc.) What are your team's strengths? What are its weaknesses? Do you feel your team will be competitive during the season? Why or why not? Be creative with your writing!

Activity 3 Manager's Log

Explain the process you used to complete a thorough statistical analysis of the players on your team. How can you tell whether or not your analysis is accurate?

Page 94 (Spanish page 136)

Your students heard about the Manager's Log in the Unit Overview, yet this will be their first experience with it. Explain that the purpose of this log is to keep a running account of the new mathematical understandings they acquire throughout the unit. Tell them that this log will help keep them and you informed of how well they are grasping the new material that is being presented to them. Let them know that it is also a way for you to identify areas where you can provide them with needed assistance.

This log can be kept either in some form of journal (composition book) or a designated area in a notebook. As an organizational tool, I recommend a clasped folder divided in two sections: one for any copied handouts and the other for notebook paper to use as the Manager's Log. This way, students have access to almost everything they need in one folder.

Be sure to have your students date each entry in their log. Let them know that each entry will be limited to between 5 and 15 minutes. After you have gone over these instructions with your students, present them with the following writing prompt either on the overhead or chalkboard:

> ***Describe the best player you feel you received in the initial draft. Use the statistical information you gathered to support your selection.***

Provide students with a quiet environment that's conducive to their fully concentrating on this writing task. Try to limit their response time to no more than 10 minutes. If time allows, you may want to have students share their responses in small groups.

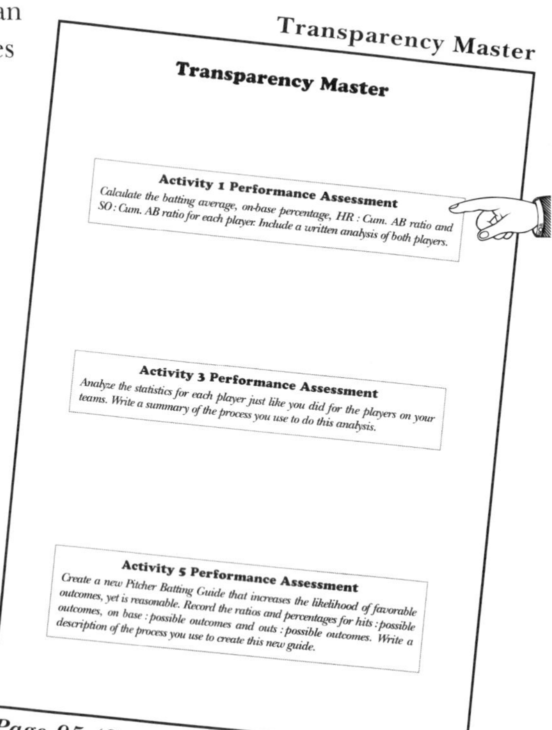
Transparency Master

Transparency Master

Activity 1 Performance Assessment

Calculate the batting average, on-base percentage, HR : Cum. AB ratio and SO : Cum. AB ratio for each player. Include a written analysis of both players.

Activity 3 Performance Assessment

Analyze the statistics for each player just like you did for the players on your teams. Write a summary of the process you use to do this analysis.

Activity 5 Performance Assessment

Create a new Pitcher Batting Guide that increases the likelihood of favorable outcomes, yet is reasonable. Record the ratios and percentages for hits : possible outcomes, on base : possible outcomes and outs : possible outcomes. Write a description of the process you use to create this new guide.

Page 95 (Spanish page 137)

Performance Assessment

Select two baseball cards (of eligible players) and provide students with the statistics from the same year. Have them calculate the batting average, on-base percentage, HR :AB ratio and SO :AB ratio for each player. Have them also include a written analysis of both players.

Looking Ahead

Let your students know that they will be working toward finalizing their rosters when they participate in trade talks and the free agent draft. Once they have solidified their teams, they will be ready to do a much more in-depth analysis of their players.

ACTIVITY 2
TRADE TALKS/FREE AGENT DRAFT

◆ ◆ ◆

Summary

Students are given a set period of time to enter into trade talks with other teams in the class. During this time they are allowed to make trades to help solidify their teams. They also participate in a free agent draft where they're given the chance to select two additional players to fill any gaps in their roster. Once their teams are complete, students fill out a final **Player Comparison Chart.**

Math Content

- statistical analysis
- determining the probability of an event
- communicating mathematically

Classroom Time

2–3 days

Materials

Transparencies:

Activity 2 Discussion Questions (The Draft — What Are Our Chances?)

Activity 2 Manager's Log

Player Comparison Charts (completed & blank)

Calculators

3" by 5" index cards

Remaining baseball cards

Manager's Log (journal)

Letter/legal size storage box

Pre-Activity Preparation

Cut up enough index cards in fourths so that each team can receive two pieces. These will be used to determine lottery selections in the Free Agent Draft.

You will want to go through your remaining baseball cards to select the 5 or 6 best players at each infield position (catcher, 1st base, 2nd base, shortstop and 3rd base) and the 12–15 best outfielders. You might want to have some interested students do this for you if you are short on time. These player cards will be available for selection in the Free Agent Draft. Be sure to have at least enough cards so that each team in the class can draft two additional players.

Trade Talks

Have your students take a look at their completed **Player Comparison Charts**. Remind them that in order to field a complete team, they will need to have the following on their roster:

catcher - 1
first baseman - 1
second baseman - 1
shortstop - 1
third baseman - 1
outfielders - 3
* **pitchers - 2**

* Students will need to select two pitchers from their selection of cards. This should not present a problem as most teams will have between 6 and 8 pitchers to choose from.

Teacher Notes

I place my free agents in notebook page card protectors (9 to a page) and post them on a bulletin board with their statistics showing. This way, the students are able to see who is available in the draft and also review their statistics in order to make decisions about who they'd like to have on their team. I remind them that they should be sure to look at each player's position as they will need to think about completing the roster for their team.

Some of your students will notice that they have an abundance of players at one position and possibly no one to play a necessary position. Explain to them that they will now be given a chance to fill any gaps they have in their roster by having a trading session with other teams, followed by a free agent draft (where they will get to select two additional players from a selection of cards that you have set aside), and then one final trading session. Upon completion of these activities, each team is expected to have a complete Major League roster of eight (8) position players and two (2) pitchers.

Before having your students begin their initial trade talks, lay out your free agent cards face down in a place where students can take a look at them but not touch them. This way, students can look at their statistics and will be aware of who will be available in the upcoming Free Agent Draft. Then inform your students that they will be given approximately 20–30 minutes for an initial trading session where they can try to complete their roster (or improve their roster if they have a complete one) by trading players with other teams. A trade can be one player for another or even several players for a (hopefully) better one. Managers should be cautioned to think carefully before making a trade as they are considered binding once cards have been exchanged.

Teacher Notes

This is an excellent time to remind students that what they are doing is selecting players in order to make tools to play a game. By making these tools and playing the game, they will be exploring mathematics that normally would be studied in a textbook, often without a context. As your students proceed through this unit, encourage them to think of ways of modifying the games (once they start them) to make them even more fun and fair for everyone involved.

During this session, students must have their completed **Player Comparison Chart** with them at all times and be prepared to share the statistics they've calculated prior to making any trade. Stress to your students that they should check a player's statistics by working them out themselves prior to making any trade. It is possible that the team they are trading with has made an error in their calculations.

Allow your students to move freely around the room to enter into trade talks. Alert them when 10 minutes have passed, 20 minutes, and when the trade talks close. Let them know that they will have one final ten minute session following the Free Agent Draft.

Free Agent Draft

Some of your students will find that they still have one or two holes in their roster following the trade talks. Explain to them that the purpose of the free agent draft is to either fill those holes or strengthen your lineup if you have no holes to fill. Let them know that each team will be allowed two free agent selections and that the order of the draft will once again be determined by a lottery.

Pass out two pieces of the cut-up index cards to each team. Tell the managers to write their team name on each piece, fold them in two and place them in a container that you carry around the room. Explain that you are going to select each of the papers at random and that for each paper chosen, the teams will be allowed to select a player from the player pool. When each paper has been removed from the container, the draft will officially be completed.

The Draft — What Are Our Chances?

Ask your students to look around the room and determine how many teams there are in the class. Explain that the purpose of this draft is to allow every team to either complete or strengthen their team in a fair way. Point out that because you are simulating a lottery, probability will affect their chances of getting the players they would like for their teams.

Have your students consider the following questions before conducting the free agent draft. You may want to have them work with their partner or in groups of four to discuss their responses.

> ***What is the probability of getting the first player selected in the draft? How did you determine this?***
>
> ***Is this probability the same for all teams? Why or why not?***
>
> ***If one of your cards is selected first, does the probability increase or decrease for having your second card selected? Explain your reasoning.***
>
> ***Do you think this lottery method is a fair way for conducting the free agent draft? If so, explain why you think it is fair. If not, why isn't it fair and what would you change to make it fair?***

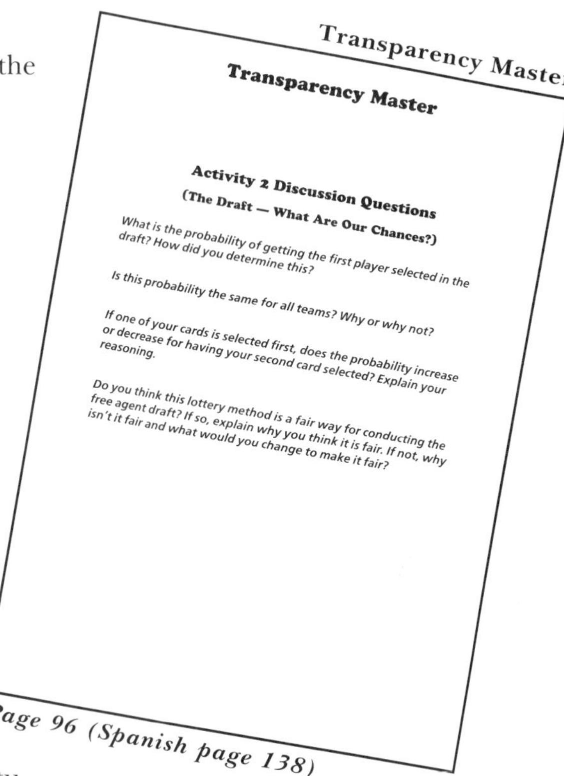

Transparency Master

Transparency Master

Activity 2 Discussion Questions
(The Draft — What Are Our Chances?)

What is the probability of getting the first player selected in the draft? How did you determine this?

Is this probability the same for all teams? Why or why not?

If one of your cards is selected first, does the probability increase or decrease for having your second card selected? Explain your reasoning.

Do you think this lottery method is a fair way for conducting the free agent draft? If so, explain why you think it is fair. If not, why isn't it fair and what would you change to make it fair?

Page 96 (Spanish page 138)

Allow your students some time to discuss and share their responses to these questions. You may even want to allow students to use the chalkboard or overhead to share the thinking that went into their responses. Although theoretically the probability is the same for all teams and it decreases for a team once one of their cards has been selected, individual students may see this process as being unfair. Try to get them to explain why it is unfair and you will find factors that are not mathematically based (other teams have better players, other managers know more, etc.). It is important for your

Teacher Notes

Sometimes, rather than telling my students how to operate the Free Agent Draft, I open up this part of the activity for my students to investigate. The question I present to them is: *How can we create a free agent draft so that it is fair to all teams involved?* Again I remind them that we are working towards playing a game and that we want the game to be fair to everyone playing. Although this investigation takes additional time, I feel that by grappling with the issue of fairness, my students gain a better understanding as a result.

students to make the distinction between mathematical fairness and other factors that skew their interpretation of what is fair and what isn't.

Explain to your students the process you will follow for the Free Agent Draft: when a card is selected and the team name is called, the managers have about 5 seconds to say which position they would like to select a card from. Each player remaining in that position pile is read aloud and the managers then have about ten seconds to make their selection. They may not look or inquire about the players' statistics at this time as this should be done prior to the draft.

After a selection is made, another card is drawn from the container. When all cards from a certain position are gone, lottery participants must select from other available positions. The draft is completed when all of the teams have been allowed to make their two selections.

Once your Free Agent Draft has been completed, ask each team to take a close look at their roster to see if any holes still remain. Again remind them that they must have a player for each of the eight (8) player positions along with their two pitchers. Tell your managers that they will have one final 10-minute trading session to make a last pitch for that special player they want to try and get from another team or to fill any position holes they may have remaining.

Teacher Notes

You would think that with all of the opportunities to make trades and draft players that every team would have a complete roster. Without fail, I always end up with one or two teams that still have a hole to fill after the final trading session. I address this small concern by keeping a small stash of average ability players at each position. When I have a team come to me that doesn't have a shortstop, for example, I give them one that I have kept aside. They cannot choose who they receive but must accept whatever card I hand them. These students are usually so excited about completing their roster that I get nothing but thanks.

Trade Talks — Final Session

Provide your students with a structured ten-minute trading session to make any last minute deals. Once this time has expired, inform your students that the player cards they now hold in their hands are the ones that will see them through the Fantasy Baseball season.

Player Comparison Chart — Final Roster

Pass out two blank **Player Comparison Charts** to each team. Tell them that they are to complete two copies of their final roster. For some of their players, they will be able to copy the statistics from their previous chart. For the new acquisitions, they will need to calculate and record the statistics. Explain to the students that each manager will need a copy of this chart to use as a resource for completing the Manager's Log entry for this activity.

Tell your students that they will be using pitchers in their upcoming games and that they should place the names of the two they've selected at the bottom of their charts. Let them know that you will be explaining the role of the pitcher as they get closer to opening the Fantasy Baseball season.

Activity Wrap — Manager's Log

Once your students have completed their final **Player Comparison Charts**, have them take out their Manager's Log (journal). Tell them to leave a small space after their last entry and enter today's date. Write the following Manager's Log writing prompt on the chalkboard or overhead:

> ***Write a letter describing your team to a real Major League team's manager (Sparky Anderson, Tommy Lasorda, etc.) What are your team's strengths? What are its weaknesses? Do you feel your team will be competitive during the season? Why or why not? Be creative with your writing!***

Transparency Master

Transparency Master

Activity 1 Manager's Log

Describe the best player you feel you received in the initial draft. Use the statistical information you gathered to support your selection.

Activity 2 Manager's Log

Write a letter describing your team to a real Major League team's manager (Sparky Anderson, Tommy Lasorda, etc.) What are your team's strengths? What are its weaknesses? Do you feel your team will be competitive during the season? Why or why not? Be creative with your writing!

Activity 3 Manager's Log

Explain the process you used to complete a thorough statistical analysis of the players on your team. How can you tell whether or not your analysis is accurate?

Page 94 (Spanish page 136)

Provide your students with 10–15 minutes of "quiet time" to reflect and write in their journals. Once they have completed their entries, have them read through their own silently, then share what they have written in small groups. If time allows, you may want to select 5 or 6 students to read their responses aloud to the whole class.

Have your students gather their Fantasy Baseball materials and place them in their team envelopes. These envelopes can then be placed in a letter/legal size storage box that sits at the front of the room. Storing the team envelopes in this type of box makes it easy for the students to retrieve and put away their materials each day without risk of forgetting or losing them.

Looking Ahead

Now that your students have finalized their rosters, it is time to move ahead with getting their players ready for the regular season. Let your students know that in the next activity, they will be learning how to do a thorough analysis of their players' statistics in order to create their player wheels. These player wheels will then be used to play the games that comprise the Fantasy Baseball season.

Activity 3
Analyzing Player Statistics

◆ ◆ ◆

Summary

Students investigate and devise a process for doing an in-depth statistical analysis of each of the position players on their teams. They discover that by using a player's cumulative at bats as the whole, they can break down each statistic to a fractional representation, convert to a decimal equivalent and finally, to the proportionate number of degrees in a circle. These calculations provide students with data they will need to create the individual player wheels in Activity 4. Students are also presented with the unit's first **Challenge Problem: Catch Him If You Can!**

Math Content

- statistical analysis
- fraction/decimal equivalence
- proportional reasoning
- multiple representations of data
- rate **(Challenge Problem #1)**
- measurement conversions **(Challenge Problem #1)**
- Pythagorean theorem (**Challenge Problem #1**)

Classroom Time

3-4 days

Materials

Student Pages:

Statistical Guide (1 per student)
Player Analysis Chart (Examples) (1 per student)
Player Analysis Chart (4 per team)
Challenge Problem #1: Catch Him If You Can! (1 per student)
Problem of the Week Procedure (1 per student)

Transparencies:

Player Analysis Chart (Examples)
Player Analysis Chart
Activity 3 Discussion Questions (How Can We Use These Player Statistics?)
Activity 3 Manager's Log
Activity 3 Performance Assessment

Robin Ventura Card transparency
Team envelopes including baseball cards
Calculators
Manager's Log (journal)

Pre-Activity Preparation

You will want to create some sample Player Wheels ahead of time to show students. You can follow the guidelines on Student Pages 103–105 that describe how to make Player Wheels.

How Can We Use These Player Statistics?

At this point, each pair of managers should now have a complete team comprised of ten baseball cards (8 position players and 2 pitchers). Remind your students that they have assembled their teams in order to create a classroom game that simulates a real baseball game. Show your students a sample player wheel and explain that these are what they will be constructing and using to play these simulated games.

Transparency Master

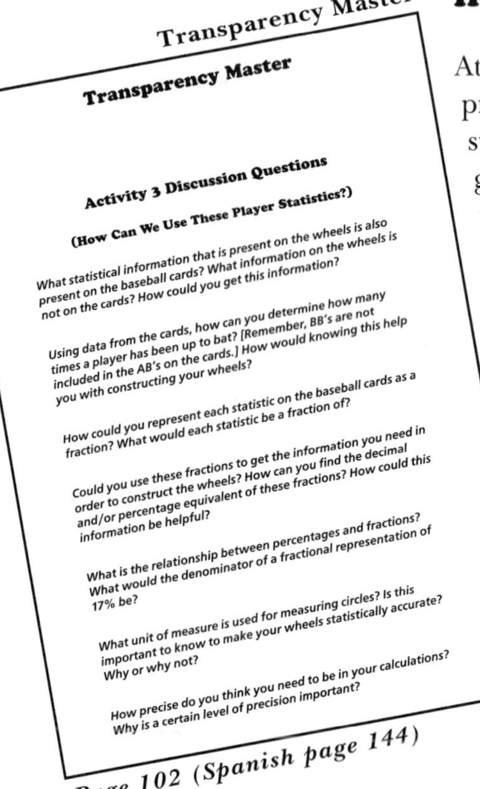

Transparency Master

Activity 3 Discussion Questions

(How Can We Use These Player Statistics?)

What statistical information that is present on the wheels is also present on the baseball cards? What information on the wheels is not on the cards? How could you get this information?

Using data from the cards, how can you determine how many times a player has been up to bat? [Remember, BB's are not included in the AB's on the cards.] How would knowing this help you with constructing your wheels?

How could you represent each statistic on the baseball cards as a fraction? What would each statistic be a fraction of?

Could you use these fractions to get the information you need in order to construct the wheels? How can you find the decimal and/or percentage equivalent of these fractions? How could this information be helpful?

What is the relationship between percentages and fractions? What would the denominator of a fractional representation of 17% be?

What unit of measure is used for measuring circles? Is this important to know to make your wheels statistically accurate? Why or why not?

How precise do you think you need to be in your calculations? Why is a certain level of precision important?

Page 102 (Spanish page 144)

Present your students with this question:

How can we use the statistics on the back of our baseball cards to make proportionately accurate player wheels?

Pass around a few sample player wheels as students grapple with this question in their small groups. After 5-10 minutes of group discussion, have students share their ideas and record them on the chalkboard or overhead for all to see.

You might want to use the following questions to assist students in their thinking about the problem you've presented.

What statistical information that is present on the wheels is also present on the baseball cards? What information on the wheels is not on the cards? How could you get this information?

Using data from the cards, how can you determine how many times a player has been up to bat? [Remember, BB's are not included in the AB's on your baseball cards.] How would knowing this help you with constructing your wheels?

How could you represent each statistic on the baseball cards as a fraction? What would each statistic be a fraction of?

Could you use these fractions to get the information you need in order to construct the wheels? How can you find the decimal and/or percentage equivalent of these fractions? How could this information be helpful?

What is the relationship between percentages and fractions? What would the denominator of a fractional representation of 17% be?

What unit of measure is used for measuring circles? Is this important to know to make your wheels statistically accurate? Why or why not?

How precise do you think you need to be in your calculations? Why is a certain level of precision important?

Student Page

FANTASY BASEBALL

Statistical Guide

This guide is intended to be used as a resource as you complete the **Player Analysis Chart** for each of your players. You will find all of the statistics you will need to complete the charts on the back of your baseball cards.

* To find **cumulative at-bats (Cum. AB)** — add the number of at-bats (AB) to the number of bases on ball (BB) shown on the card.
* To find **singles (1B)** — subtract the number of doubles (2B), triples (3B) and home runs (HR) from the number of hits (H) shown on the card.
* To determine **Other Outs** — add the hits (H), bases on balls (BB) and strike outs (SO) and subtract the total from the **Cum. AB**.
* To determine **Fly Outs (FO)** and **Ground Outs (GO)** — divide the number of **Other Outs** by 2. The quotient goes under each heading **(FO)** and **(GO)**.

  Example: $\frac{\text{Other Outs}}{142}$ $\frac{142}{2}$ $\frac{\text{FO}}{71}$ $\frac{\text{GO}}{71}$

  (If Other Outs yields an odd number, increase either Fly Outs or Ground Outs by 1.)
* To represent the **Ratio of a Statistic to Cum. AB** as a fraction — record the Cum. AB total as the denominator and the value of each statistic as the numerator.
* To determine the **Decimal Equivalent** — divide the numerator by the denominator. Record only to the fourth (4th) decimal place.

  Example: $\frac{\text{1B}}{\text{Cum. AB}} = \frac{109}{551} = .1978$
* To determine the **Degrees** — multiply the decimal equivalent for each statistic by **360** (number of degrees in a circle). Round each product to the nearest whole number.

  Example: $.1978 \times 360 = 71.208$ or 71 degrees

Page 97 (Spanish page 139)

As students think about these questions and share their responses, you may want to assist them in organizing their thoughts. You can either have them create their own methods for finding the necessary data to construct their player wheels, develop a group method for doing this, or use what they have investigated to lead them into the next section. The choice is up to you!

A Tool — Player Analysis Charts

Your students have probably generated a number of ideas for analyzing the statistics on the back of their players' cards. If you are electing to use the following guides to assist in this analysis, explain to your students that this is one method that can be used to gather needed data for creating their player wheels. Have your students pull out the baseball cards from their team envelopes. Have them set the pitcher cards aside as they will not need them at this time. Explain to your students that they will be able to use the statistical data on the baseball cards for any year in which a player had 200+ AB's for a Major League team.

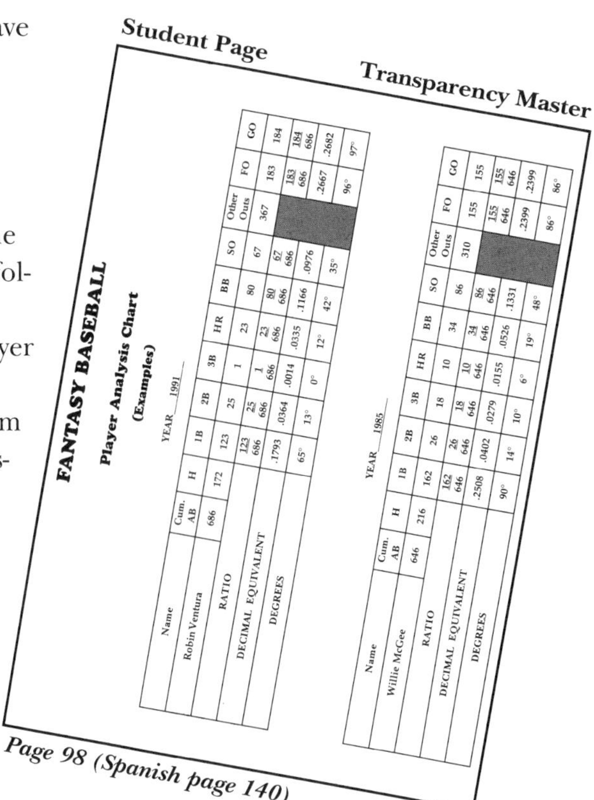
Student Page — Transparency Master

FANTASY BASEBALL
Player Analysis Chart
(Examples)

YEAR 1991

Name	Cum. AB	H	1B	2B	3B	HR	BB	SO	Other Outs	FO	GO
Robin Ventura	686	172	123	25	1	23	80	67	367	183	184
RATIO			123/686	25/686	1/686	23/686	80/686	67/686		183/686	184/686
DECIMAL EQUIVALENT			.1793	.0364	.0014	.0335	.1166	.0976		.2667	.2682
DEGREES			65°	13°	0°	12°	42°	35°		96°	97°

YEAR 1985

Name	Cum. AB	H	1B	2B	3B	HR	BB	SO	Other Outs	FO	GO
Willie McGee	646	216	162	26	18	10	34	86	310	155	155
RATIO			162/646	26/646	18/646	10/646	34/646	86/646		155/646	155/646
DECIMAL EQUIVALENT			.2508	.0402	.0279	.0155	.0526	.1331		.2399	.2399
DEGREES			90°	14°	10°	6°	19°	48°		86°	86°

Page 98 (Spanish page 140)

Pass out 2 copies of the **Statistical Guide** and the **Player Analysis Chart (Examples)** as well as 4 blank copies of the **Player Analysis Chart** to each team. Walk your students through the Robin Ventura example on the **Player Analysis Chart (Examples),** referring to the **Robin Ventura Card** and the **Statistical Guide** to explain how the numbers were arrived at. Your students will discover that there are FO's (fly outs) and GO's (ground outs) on the charts yet these statistics cannot be found on the baseball cards. Explain that because we don't have information about how the players made their outs, a decision was made to split the numbers evenly between these two categories.

As you proceed through your example (using the **Statistical Guide** as a resource), be sure to point out what method is being used. You may also want to point out that Robin Ventura has 1 triple but this shows up on the **Player Analysis Chart** as 0°. Have students discuss why they think this is so. Keep asking your students questions: what data do you need, how can you write the ratios as fractions, how can you find the decimal equivalent and degrees for each statistic. You want them to be thinking and connecting all of this as you work through the example together.

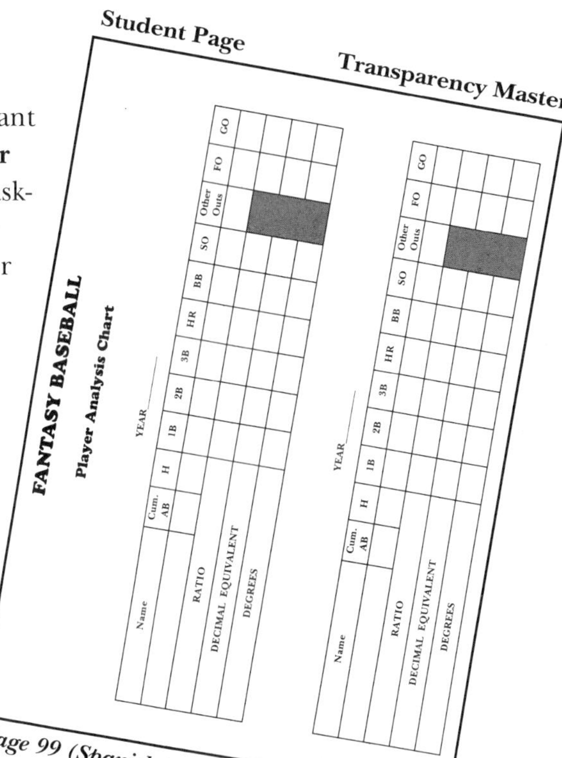
Student Page — Transparency Master

FANTASY BASEBALL
Player Analysis Chart

YEAR ____

Name	Cum. AB	H	1B	2B	3B	HR	BB	SO	Other Outs	FO	GO
RATIO											
DECIMAL EQUIVALENT											
DEGREES											

YEAR ____

Name	Cum. AB	H	1B	2B	3B	HR	BB	SO	Other Outs	FO	GO
RATIO											
DECIMAL EQUIVALENT											
DEGREES											

Page 99 (Spanish page 141)

Before having students fill out charts for their own cards, you may want them to discuss the statistics for Willie McGee on the **Player Analysis Chart (Examples).** Ask them if, given the 1985 statistics, they think the ratios, decimal equivalents, and degrees are accurate. How can they check these numbers? Investigating this example will help students get additional practice in making connections between ratios, decimals, and degrees.

Player Analysis Charts — On Their Own

After you walk through an example or two with your students and field any questions they have, they should be ready to complete the **Player Analysis Charts** using their players' statistics. Emphasize the importance of accuracy as these charts will be used to create their player wheels. A quick way for your students to check for accuracy is to total the values they have for degrees. Their total for each player should equal 360 degrees. Your students will find that if completed accurately, their totals for degrees will range from 358 to 362. Ask your students why they think that this sometimes occurs and whether or not they think it is acceptable. If someone does not identify the reason, point out that this occurs because of rounding the degrees to the nearest whole number. As a class, decide on a process that you will use when this happens so that the totals can be adjusted to equal precisely 360 degrees.

Teacher Notes

I love when this comes up because it lends itself to a great discussion about precision. Although I don't want students to necessarily go back and do their calculations over, we can talk about the fact that measurement is not precise. Usually, we make an agreement that if you need to add 1 or 2 degrees to total 360, these are added to the singles. If they need to subtract 1 or 2 degrees, they are subtracted from one of the out categories. I have found this to be an equitable method for dealing with this dilemma.

Your students will most likely need more than one class period to complete their charts. Unless you want to assign this as homework, be prepared to allow for some additional time at the beginning of the next class period.

Ongoing Sponge Activity — Designing Baseball Cards

Once your students get going on this activity, you'll find that they work at different speeds and will finish at different times. For this reason, it is good to have an on-going task that students can go back to whenever they have some spare time on their hands. The following task can be presented to students before getting into the main activity. You may want to allow some time for students to get started with this task before continuing with the activity.

Present your students with the following task:

> ***Design your very own Major League baseball card with you as the star player. Make your card as realistic as possible by including all of the information you find on a real baseball card. Do not copy the statistics from an original baseball card but rather create your own statistics that may be excellent, yet reasonable.***

Tell your students that they can work on this task anytime they find themselves with some extra time. Have the students use half of a sheet of 8 ½" by 11" white cardstock for their cards. This will make it easier for them to record the statistics on back. You can do a number of things with these cards: start a "Wall of Fame," laminate them and hang them from the ceiling above the students' desks, place them in a binder for a manager's record, etc.

Teacher Notes

I personally like to make a "Wall of Fame" with the cards that my students construct. I laminate each card and fasten them to the wall in a way that allows the viewer to lift the card and read the stats on the back. I have ended up with some pretty incredible looking cards in the past with some phenomenal, yet realistic statistics. Sometimes I give students an additional assignment to write a short, (hypothetical) biographical sketch that pertains to their cards. This allows my creative writers to run wild and weave their own historical data that supports the statistics they've included on their cards.

Player Analysis Charts — Quality Control

Remind your students that they are getting ready to enter into a simulated baseball season that will undoubtedly become quite competitive. If you also happen to be dangling a possible Division Pennant and World Series Championship in front of your students, you will definitely want to avoid any controversy. For this reason, I require each team to check one other team's **Player Analysis Charts.** This check is done in order to catch any unintentional mistakes along with any intentional attempts at gaining an unfair advantage.

Depending on how much time you feel you have to spare, you can have your students check another team's charts by:

A) Checking every statistic and calculation for each player

or

B) Checking the total number of degrees — making sure they total exactly 360.

Whichever option you choose, be sure to encourage your students to be as thorough as possible. Let them know that this will be the only student quality control check on these charts.

Your students will finish with their charts at all different times. Once their charts have been completed and they have had them checked by another team and checked another team's charts, remind them about completing their baseball cards. You can also use students that are finished as resources to assist others if needed.

Student Page

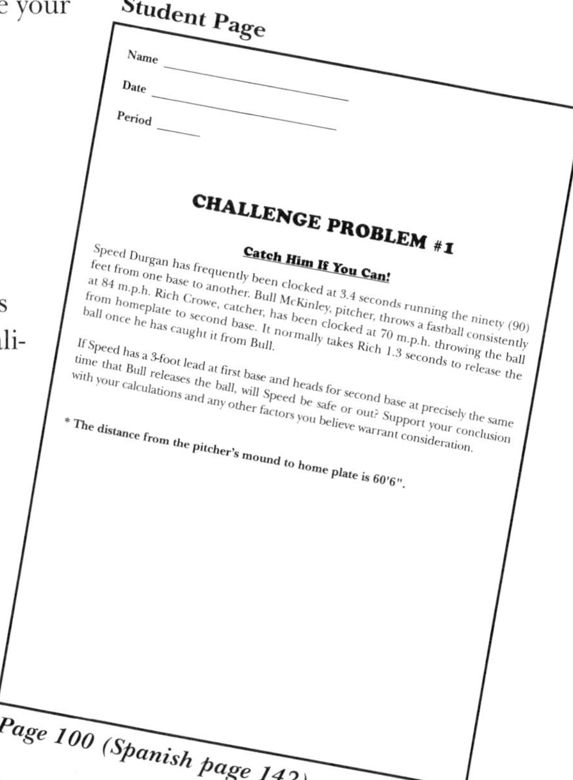

Name

Date

Period

CHALLENGE PROBLEM #1

Catch Him If You Can!

Speed Durgan has frequently been clocked at 3.4 seconds running the ninety (90) feet from one base to another. Bull McKinley, pitcher, throws a fastball consistently at 84 m.p.h. Rich Crowe, catcher, has been clocked at 70 m.p.h. throwing the ball from homeplate to second base. It normally takes Rich 1.3 seconds to release the ball once he has caught it from Bull.

If Speed has a 3-foot lead at first base and heads for second base at precisely the same time that Bull releases the ball, will Speed be safe or out? Support your conclusion with your calculations and any other factors you believe warrant consideration.

*** The distance from the pitcher's mound to home plate is 60'6".**

Page 100 (Spanish page 142)

Challenge Problem #1 — Catch Him If You Can

This is a nice spot to present your students with the first of three Challenge Problems created specifically for this unit. Challenge problems are included in this unit to provide students with opportunities to flex their mathematical thinking. They are rich mathematical problems written within the context of baseball. They are useful as they require students to apply mathematical concepts they have learned in a real world situation. Along with this, they are expected to communicate in writing the processes they use and the reasoning that supports their solution. These problems can be used strictly within the confines of the classroom or assigned to be done outside of class as a homework activity. Regardless of how you use them, I encourage you to first work through them on your own or with your colleagues. Get together and share your solutions, your strategies, and your reasoning. This process will help to identify the understandings you want your students to gain from experiencing these problems. Some further information about how to process this Challenge Problem and some questions you might use to stimulate student thinking is given at the beginning of Activity 5 (page 42).

This challenge problem, **Catch Him If You Can**, requires students to convert units of measure, apply the Pythagorean Theorem to find the distance from home plate to second base, and use logical reasoning to arrive at a solution. Students also consider velocity, trajectory, precision, and other factors that may influence their response to the problem. This problem does not have a clear-cut solution as the runner can legitimately be called safe or out depending on the reasoning provided by the students. What is important is that students work with the mathematical concepts that will help them formulate and defend their solution to the problem.

Student Page

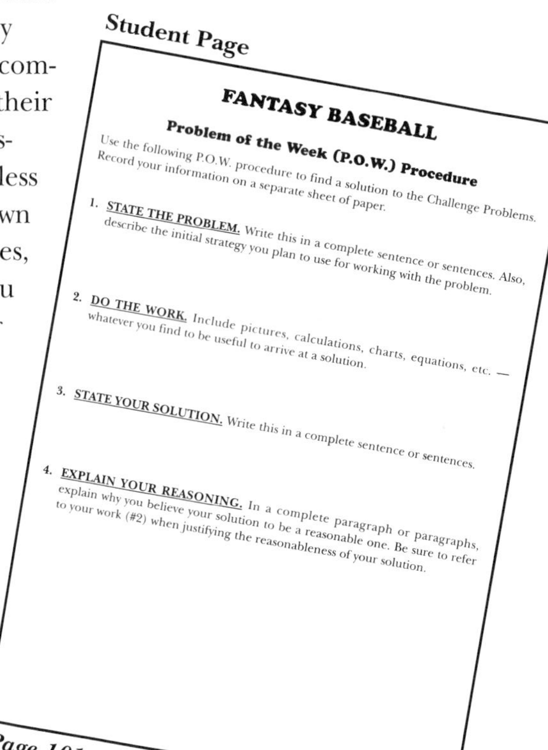

FANTASY BASEBALL

Problem of the Week (P.O.W.) Procedure

Use the following P.O.W. procedure to find a solution to the Challenge Problems. Record your information on a separate sheet of paper.

1. STATE THE PROBLEM. Write this in a complete sentence or sentences. Also, describe the initial strategy you plan to use for working with the problem.
2. DO THE WORK. Include pictures, calculations, charts, equations, etc. — whatever you find to be useful to arrive at a solution.
3. STATE YOUR SOLUTION. Write this in a complete sentence or sentences.
4. EXPLAIN YOUR REASONING. In a complete paragraph or paragraphs, explain why you believe your solution to be a reasonable one. Be sure to refer to your work (#2) when justifying the reasonableness of your solution.

Page 101 (Spanish page 143)

Transparency Master

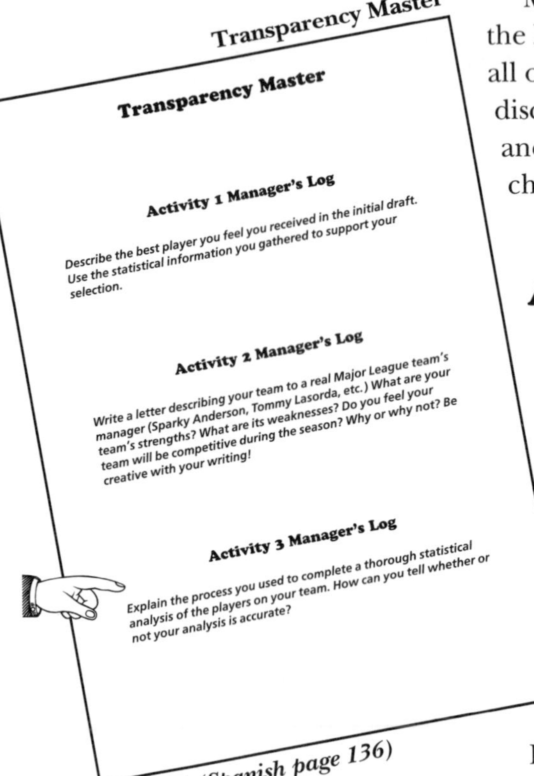
Transparency Master

Activity 1 Manager's Log

Describe the best player you feel you received in the initial draft. Use the statistical information you gathered to support your selection.

Activity 2 Manager's Log

Write a letter describing your team to a real Major League team's manager (Sparky Anderson, Tommy Lasorda, etc.) What are your team's strengths? What are its weaknesses? Do you feel your team will be competitive during the season? Why or why not? Be creative with your writing!

Activity 3 Manager's Log

Explain the process you used to complete a thorough statistical analysis of the players on your team. How can you tell whether or not your analysis is accurate?

Page 94 (Spanish page 136)

Make sure that every student has a copy of **Challenge Problem #1** as well as the **Problem of the Week (P.O.W.) Procedure** sheet. Tell your students to show all of their work on a separate sheet of paper and to be prepared to share and discuss their conclusions in class in a week. Encourage them to work together and talk with each other outside of class while working on a solution to this challenge problem.

Activity Wrap — Manager's Log

Once your students have completed their **Player Analysis Charts**, have them staple the sheets together, then collect them for your review. Tell the students that they will be returned prior to their beginning the next activity.

Have your students take out their Manager's Log for this activity's entry. On your overhead or chalkboard, write the following:

Explain the process you used to complete a thorough statistical analysis of the players on your team. How can you tell whether or not your analysis is accurate?

Provide your students with roughly 5–10 minutes of "quiet time" to complete this entry in their log. If time allows, have them share their writing in small groups and possibly select a few to share with the class.

Transparency Master

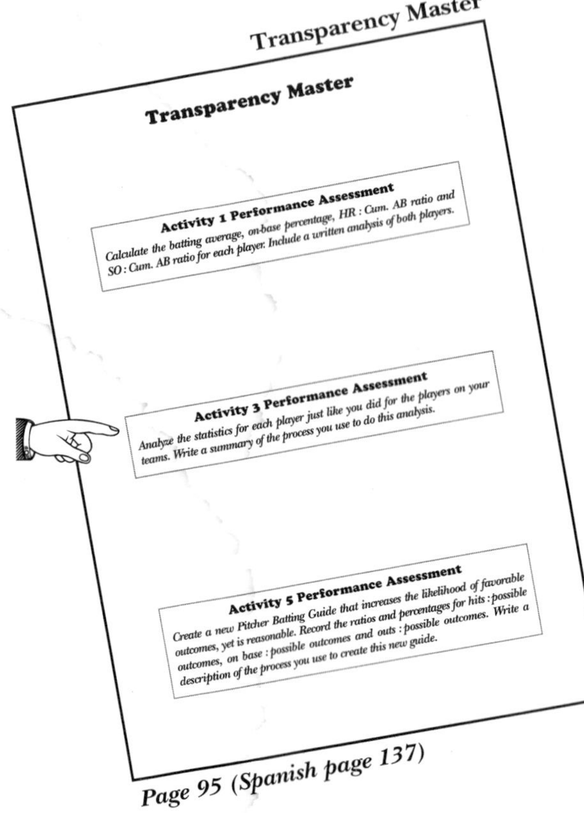
Transparency Master

Activity 1 Performance Assessment

Calculate the batting average, on-base percentage, HR : Cum. AB ratio and SO : Cum. AB ratio for each player. Include a written analysis of both players.

Activity 3 Performance Assessment

Analyze the statistics for each player just like you did for the players on your teams. Write a summary of the process you use to do this analysis.

Activity 5 Performance Assessment

Create a new Pitcher Batting Guide that increases the likelihood of favorable outcomes, yet is reasonable. Record the ratios and percentages for hits : possible outcomes, on base : possible outcomes and outs : possible outcomes. Write a description of the process you use to create this new guide.

Page 95 (Spanish page 137)

Performance Assessment

Present students with the statistics off the back of a baseball card for any eligible player. Be sure to select a year with at least 200 AB's. Ask students to complete an analysis of these statistics similar to what they did for the players on their teams. Have them include a written summary of the process they used to do this analysis.

Looking Ahead

Tell your students that they are getting very close to completing all of the necessary prep work that needs to be done prior to opening the season. Let them know that in the next activity, they will be making the player wheels that they will be using for the simulated games.

ACTIVITY 4
CONSTRUCTING PLAYER WHEELS

◆ ◆ ◆

Summary

Students use their completed **Player Analysis Charts** for designing the player wheels to be used in the simulated games. They discuss the various possibilities of placement on the wheels of the different statistics and whether or not placement would have any bearing on the probability of an outcome. They also complete a quality control check of another team's player wheels.

Math Content

- logical reasoning
- angle measure (circle graphs)
- proportional reasoning
- predicting the probability of an event
- collecting, organizing, interpreting and analyzing data

Classroom Time

3–4 days

Materials

Student Pages:

  How to Make a Player Wheel (1 per student)
  How to Make a Player Wheel (pictorial model) (1 per student)
  Making Spinners (1 per student)
  Player Wheel Master (6 per team)

Transparencies:

  Activity 4 Manager's Log

Player Analysis Chart (Examples) Transparency
Player Analysis Charts (completed)
Cardstock (2 different colors — approx. 100 sheets of each)
Colored pencils or markers
Compasses (optional)
Protractors (1 per student)
Scissors (1 pair per student)
Paper clips (small)
Masking tape
Manager's Log

Pre-Activity Preparation

Make sure you have enough of one color of cardstock so that each team can receive 6 sheets. With the other cardstock, you will need to run off copies of the **Player Wheels** student page. Each team will need6 copies of this as well. If you prefer to have your students construct the circles for their wheels, you won't need the **Player Wheels** student page.

Teacher Notes

I always use light colored cardstock for making the wheels. This way, the students can be creative with their wheel designs and not be concerned with whether or not the colors they use for designing the base of their wheels will show up. Light blue, canary yellow and cream seem to work best and are usually easy to find. The exact colors don't matter but you should try to find two different colors so students can make the wheels one color and the base of the wheels another color.

Constructing A Player Wheel — Demonstration

Prior to passing out materials and turning your students loose to design their player wheels, I suggest that you demonstrate a procedure for making the wheels. The 10–15 minutes that you'll spend at the start of class will save you a great deal of time and trouble answering countless questions. Again, this places the responsibility of paying close attention and asking clarifying questions on the shoulders of your students.

There are several ways that you can demonstrate the actual construction of the player wheel. You can use the methods shown on the student pages titled **How to Make a Player Wheel** and **Making Spinners** (pages 103–105) or use a method for making spinners that you prefer. Regardless of how you model this, your students will undoubtedly develop their own unique methods for constructing their wheels. This should be encouraged at all times.

Does Placement Affect Probability?

When you demonstrated how to make a wheel, you undoubtedly placed the statistics in some kind of order. You may have placed them in the order that they appeared on the **Player Analysis Chart** or you may have placed them randomly. Regardless of what method you used, it is time to present your students with a question that will lead them into an interesting investigation.

Hold up the wheel you just constructed and point out to your students that they will be using wheels to play the simulated baseball games. Explain that by spinning the wheels, they will be able to determine what a player does each time they go to bat. The results will then be recorded on a scoresheet just as if the players were playing an actual game. Reinforce the idea that these wheels are a visual representation of the data found on the **Player Analysis Charts.**

Student Page

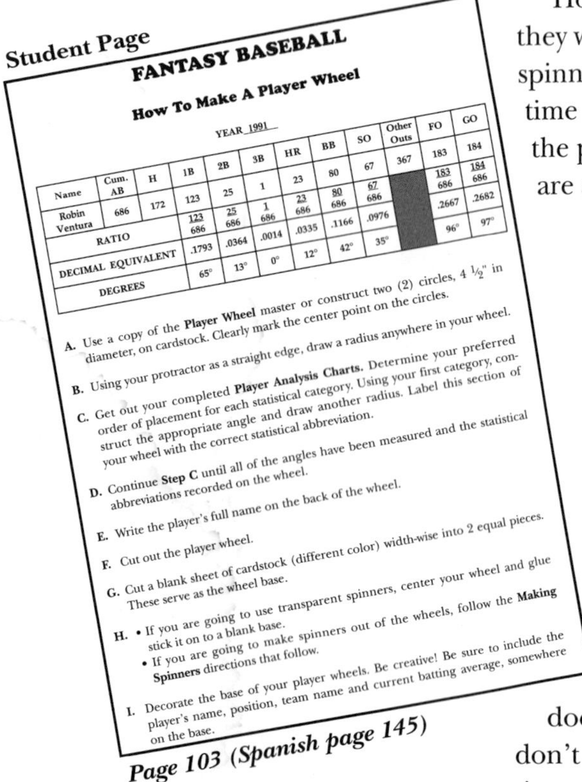

FANTASY BASEBALL

How To Make A Player Wheel

YEAR 1991

Name	Cum. AB	H	1B	2B	3B	HR	BB	SO	Other Outs	FO	GO
Robin Ventura	686	172	123	25	1	23	80	67	367	183	184
RATIO			123/686	25/686	1/686	23/686	80/686	67/686		183/686	184/686
DECIMAL EQUIVALENT			.1793	.0364	.0014	.0335	.1166	.0976		.2667	.2682
DEGREES			65°	13°	0°	12°	42°	35°		96°	97°

A. Use a copy of the **Player Wheel** master or construct two (2) circles, 4 ½" in diameter, on cardstock. Clearly mark the center point on the circles.

B. Using your protractor as a straight edge, draw a radius anywhere in your wheel.

C. Get out your completed **Player Analysis Charts.** Determine your preferred order of placement for each statistical category. Using your first category, construct the appropriate angle and draw another radius. Label this section of your wheel with the correct statistical abbreviation.

D. Continue **Step C** until all of the angles have been measured and the statistical abbreviations recorded on the wheel.

E. Write the player's full name on the back of the wheel.

F. Cut out the player wheel.

G. Cut a blank sheet of cardstock (different color) width-wise into 2 equal pieces. These serve as the wheel base.

H. • If you are going to use transparent spinners, center your wheel and glue stick it on to a blank base.
• If you are going to make spinners out of the wheels, follow the **Making Spinners** directions that follow.

I. Decorate the base of your player wheels. Be creative! Be sure to include the player's name, position, team name and current batting average, somewhere on the base.

Page 103 (Spanish page 145)

Present the following questions to your students:

Do you think the order you place the statistics on the wheel will have any effect on the outcome of a certain number of spins? Why or why not? Try to convince someone that disagrees with you to change their way of thinking and agree with yours.

Give your students an opportunity to think about this question, discuss their thoughts in small groups and share with the class. Try to limit this discussion to 10–15 minutes as you are going to have students investigate whether or not placement affects the probability of outcomes. At the end of this time you will have a segment of your classroom population that is convinced placement affects probability while the others are certain it does not. A great question to ask is: **"How can we find out?"** If your students don't come up with the idea of running an experiment, you may want to ask questions to help them arrive at this idea.

Have a discussion with your students that clarifies which statistics on the wheels yield favorable outcomes (1B, 2B, 3B, HR, BB — they allow a batter to reach base), and which statistics yield unfavorable outcomes (SO, FO, GO) and why these are unfavorable (make an out). Explain that in order to maintain some consistency in their experiment, they are going to look at two different methods of placing the statistics on the wheels, *clumping* and *spreading*. A wheel that is *clumped* has all of the favorable outcomes placed together and all of the unfavorable outcomes placed together. A wheel that is *spread* has the favorable outcomes mixed in with the unfavorable outcomes. (See examples below.)

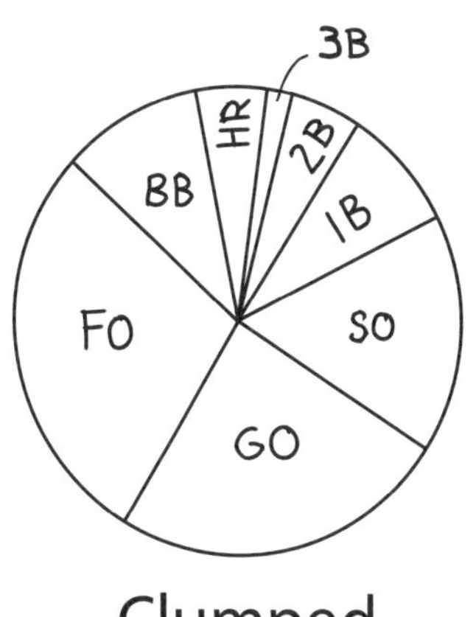

Clumped

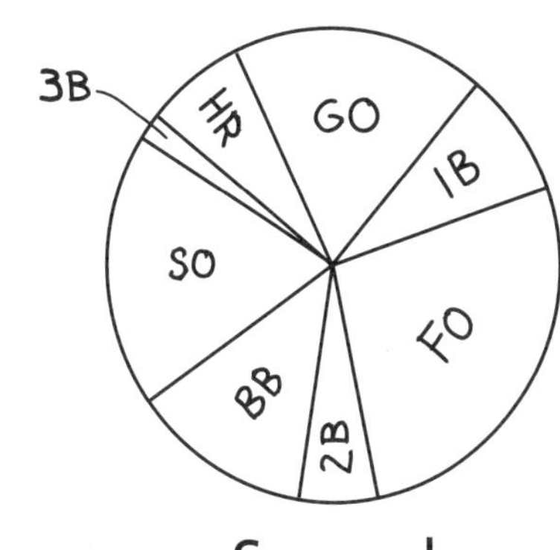

Spread

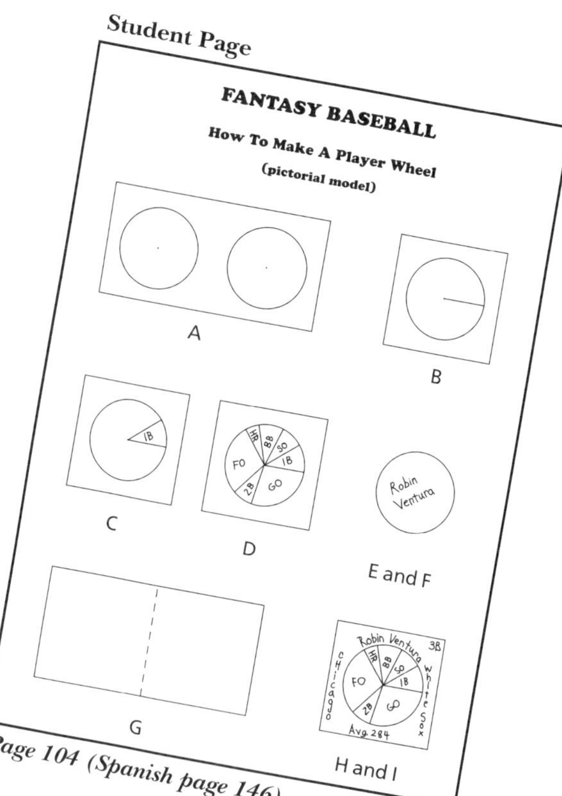

Page 104 (Spanish page 146)

Point out to students the Willie McGee example on the **Player Analysis Chart (Examples)** transparency. Tell your students that each of them will use the degrees from this chart to construct a player wheel that will either be clumped or spread. In order to gather enough data, you will want to have the same number of samples for each type of wheel. One way of ensuring this is to have one co-manager of a team make a clumped wheel and the other co-manager make a spread wheel. Pass out the materials necessary for each student to create one player wheel, including the student pages **How To Make a Player Wheel, How to Make a Player Wheel (pictorial model), Making Spinners**, and the **Player Wheel Master** sheet. As this is the first player wheel your students will be making, expect some additional questions.

Once the wheels have been constructed, have the students make a tally sheet to record the results of 50 spins. Before having them spin their wheels and record their results, ask:

Is there anything we need to consider before starting this experiment?

Some of the points you will want to discuss with your students are what constitutes a spin and what you will do as a group about spins that land on a line. You might want to present the following to your students:

A spin is considered acceptable if the wheel makes a minimum of one complete revolution.

If after completing a spin, the wheel lands on a line, the wheel is spun over.

Teacher Notes

One of my students once suggested that if the wheel landed on the line, the better of the two statistics should be taken. This led to a great discussion about whether this presented an unfair advantage to one group or the other. What do you think, does it? Talk about it with your students.

Once you've decided on all of the parameters, have each student spin his or her wheel 50 times and tally the results. While they are doing this, post two charts (see samples below) at the front of the room. As students finish their spins, have them record their results on the appropriate chart.

	CLUMPED								SPREAD							
	1B	2B	3B	HR	BB	SO	FO	GO	1B	2B	3B	HR	BB	SO	FO	GO
TOTAL																
	Favorable Outcomes					Unfavorable Outcomes			Favorable Outcomes					Unfavorable Outcomes		

Student Page

FANTASY BASEBALL

Making Spinners

1. Estimate the center of the base. lightly mark a point at the center. Using a straight edge, draw a dark, thin line from the center point to the lower left corner.
2. Cut out three 1" by 1" squares from the paper scraps left from cutting out the wheels.
3. Bend your paper clip so that the smaller, inside loop bends up. Pull the end of the this loop up to expose the pointed end. Use this point to poke holes in the center of the wheel and center point of the base.
4. Put bent paper clip through the center hole of the base (clip goes up through the bottom). The large loop of the paper clip should lay flat along the bottom of the base.
5. Place your three paper squares (washers) and then your wheel over the paper clip and on top of the base. Bend the paper clip down.
6. Put masking tape on the bottom to hold the paper clip flush against the base.

Base

Wheel

Base

Washers

Tape

Page 105 (Spanish page 147)

Once all students have posted their results on the charts, give them some time to look at and discuss the results of their experiment. More than likely they will see disparity in the results from sample to sample. With the results posted in this way, it may or may not be easy for them to draw conclusions that will support or negate their original prediction. Totaling each statistic for each chart helps to bring the data into clearer focus. This way they will not only be able to compare the results of each statistic, they'll be able to compare favorable outcomes to unfavorable outcomes.

Theoretically, the placement of the statistics should have no bearing on the probability of the different outcomes. With a large sample of trials and the random spinning of wheels, the results should be relatively close in number. In the classroom, however, there is sometimes a question about whether or not the wheels are being spun randomly. Students get into a groove where the same statistics are spun several times in a row. You may want to use this phenomenon as a springboard for a discussion of the role of fairness in probability.

After discussing the results of your experiment, tell students to feel free to use this information when they begin constructing player wheels for their teams. Also, tell your students to hold on to their sample player wheels as they will be using them to further investigate probability as the unit progresses.

Constructing Player Wheels

Once you feel that your students are ready to go off on their own and construct their player wheels, provide them with the time and materials necessary to complete the task. Tell them to be very careful with their measurements as it is no fun to have to go back and reconstruct a player wheel due to inaccurate measurements. Suggest to them that they lightly sketch their lines on the wheels and make sure they are all accurate before darkening them.

How your students decide to place the statistics on the wheels should be left entirely up to them. They do not need to clump all of their wheels or spread all of them but rather may choose to vary from wheel to wheel. What's important is that they reach agreement with their co-manager before proceeding with construction.

Stress to your class that every student needs not only to be involved in the construction of the wheels, but also to be willing to assist anyone who may have a question or need help. Tell them that a cooperative atmosphere needs to be present in the classroom at this time — they will have plenty of time to be competitive in the near future!

Once again, remind your students that their completed wheels are visual representations of their players' statistics recorded on the **Player Analysis Charts**. Mention that they should be able to check these charts and make a visual comparison of the wheels to tell who are the consistent hitters, power hitters, strikeout kings, etc. They should also be able to compare the wheels with the charts to make sure each section of the wheel is proportionately accurate.

As your students construct their wheels, they may find that the last angle they measure never seems to be accurate. This is a great opportunity to discuss with your students, the impreciseness of measurement. Knowing that this often happens, you may want to ask them whether they think the last statistic measured should be one that is favorable or unfavorable.

Player Wheels — Quality Control

As with the **Player Analysis Charts**, each team is expected to conduct a quality control check on another team's player wheels. It is crucial that each team do a thorough check of each wheel as this is the only time these are checked. Let your students know that angle measure mistakes could possibly change the outcome of a game and that accuracy is extremely important in order to be fair to everyone involved. With each co-manager checking four (4) of another team's wheels, this quality control check should take no more than fifteen or twenty minutes to complete.

Teacher Notes

It will take time for your students to complete these player wheels to their satisfaction. Be patient — this is time well spent as they argue placement, investigate probabilities, measure with precision, reason and communicate mathematically, as well as be creative. This is actually a great time for you to go around the classroom with a video camera!

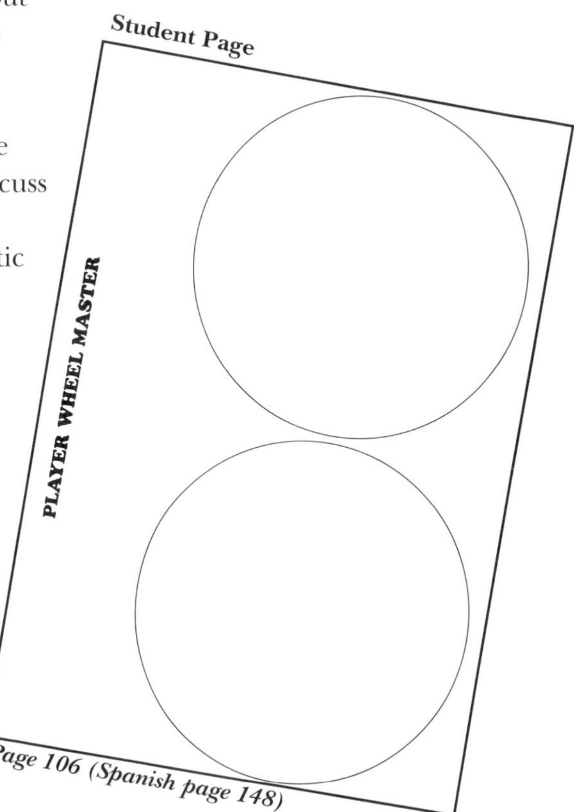

You will find that each of your teams will finish at a different pace. Those students that have completed their tasks prior to the end of the allotted time should be encouraged to work on **Challenge Problem #1,** experiment with their new player wheels, work on their individual baseball card, continue to decorate their team envelope or assist other groups that could use their assistance.

Teacher Notes

I have always been pleased with the results from the student responses to this writing prompt. Most have maintained an extremely high level of interest despite the fact that they haven't gotten into the "fun" part yet — the actual playing of the games. There are always a few students who are not thrilled with what they are doing and others that enjoy some of what they're doing and dislike other parts. Reading this entry helps me to see which students I need to provide with additional support and encouragement.

Activity Wrap — Manager's Log

Tell your students that their **Manager's Log** entry is going to be slightly different today. Tell them that they are going to have 10–15 minutes to write to the following:

My impression of Fantasy Baseball, so far . . .

Encourage your students to write using a style that is comfortable to them. Stress the importance of being honest with themselves and with you regarding what they think about the unit so far. Ask them to be as specific and descriptive as possible regarding what they like and dislike. Let them know that their input will assist you as you take them through the rest of the unit.

Provide your students with 10–15 minutes of "quiet time" to complete this entry in their log. If time allows, have them share their writing in small groups and possibly call on a few interested students to share with the class.

Looking Ahead

Inform your students that tomorrow they will begin learning how to use their player wheels to play the actual Fantasy Baseball game. They will be learning how to keep score of a game by participating in a simulation. They will also have the opportunity to challenge a team of their choice to a practice game.

Transparency Master

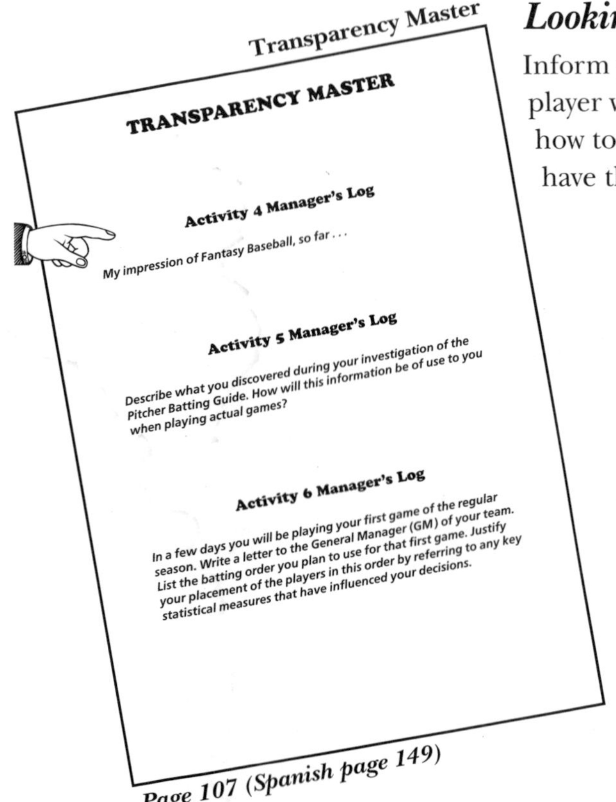

TRANSPARENCY MASTER

Activity 4 Manager's Log

My impression of Fantasy Baseball, so far . . .

Activity 5 Manager's Log

Describe what you discovered during your investigation of the Pitcher Batting Guide. How will this information be of use to you when playing actual games?

Activity 6 Manager's Log

In a few days you will be playing your first game of the regular season. Write a letter to the General Manager (GM) of your team. List the batting order you plan to use for that first game. Justify your placement of the players in this order by referring to any key statistical measures that have influenced your decisions.

Page 107 (Spanish page 149)

Activity 5
Playing the Game/Instruction

◆ ◆ ◆

Summary

Students are introduced to the actual Fantasy Baseball game. They get actively involved as they represent base runners while a simulated game is played using a team's player wheels. Students receive instruction on how to keep score of a game and compile statistics at the end of a game. Students are also given an opportunity to play a practice game against another team. At the conclusion of their games, students investigate the criteria presented to them regarding pitchers and their chances for reaching base safely.

Math Content

- collecting, organizing, interpreting and analyzing data
- calculating ratios, percentages, averages
- combinations/permutations
- determining the probability of an event

Classroom Time

2–3 days

Materials

Student Pages:

Scorekeeping Guide 1 per student)
Pitcher Batting Guide (1 per student)
Sample Scoresheet (1 per student)
Scoresheets (blank - 2 per team)

Transparencies:

Scorekeeping Guide
Pitcher Batting Guide
Scoresheet (blank)
Sample Scoresheet
Activity 5 Discussion Questions (Investigating the Pitcher Batting Guide)

Activity 5 Manager's Log transparency
Activity 5 Performance Assessment transparency
Player wheels (1 set per team)
Dice (1 pair per team)
Calculators
Manager's Log (journal)

Pre-Activity Preparation

You will want to study the **Sample Scoresheet** and familiarize yourself with the procedure for scoring a game. Also, set up a simulated baseball diamond in your classroom. This will be used by the students as they actually act out the course of a game. You may want to bring in real bases or use paper to represent them.

A Return to Challenge Problem #1 — Processing the Math

Before you have your students begin scoring and playing games, you will want to go back to Challenge Problem #1 and have your students share their solutions, strategies, and reasoning. I usually have my students share first in small groups, usually of 3 to 4 students. During this sharing, everyone is expected to be an active listener and ask questions that will help clarify a presenter's thinking and reasoning. Afterwards, each group is expected to work together to prepare a group response to be shared with t he class. The idea here is to compile the strengths from each group member's paper and prepare a group response to be presented to the class. I usually have half of the groups present but if time allows or if I feel there is still more to be brought out in the problem, I allow time for the other groups to present.

The following questions are provided to assist you with processing this Challenge Problem with your students. You may choose to present your students with some of these questions as they are grappling with the problem or strictly use them to process the problem upon completion. These questions are not all-inclusive — while working through the problem you may discover others that would be of benefit to your students. Write them down and use them.

What is the distance that Speed needs to cover to get from first to second? How long will it take him to get there? What process did you use to figure this out?

How long does it take for the ball to get to Rich once it leaves Bull's hand? How did you determine this?

What is the distance the ball needs to travel to get from Rich to second base? How did you determine this distance? How long will it take the ball to get to second base once it leaves Rich's hand? How did you determine this amount of time?

Who/what will reach second base first, Speed or the ball? What is the time difference between the two? Is this a significant amount of time? Why or why not?

What factors did you consider when determining your solution? How did these factors enter into your decision? Are there any that you initially considered, then dismissed? If so, what were they and why did you dismiss them?

Is this a good problem? Why or why not?

Teacher Notes

After the class presentations, I have my students turn their individual and group papers in to me. I review the group papers and award group credit based on a generic 4-point rubric created at the beginning of the school year by my students. I read through the individual papers, then shuffle them and set them aside for a class scoring session to be done the following week.

The process for the class scoring session that I use is as follows: Each group receives a random set of 4 papers. Each group member reads and scores all 4 papers using the same scoring rubric used for the group papers. These scores are recorded on a half sheet of paper along with any comments the scorers may wish to include. This half sheet of paper is then stapled to the original paper and the papers are then returned to the original owners, reviewed, and placed in the students' portfolios.

Reviewing Scorekeeping Guides

Now that your students have constructed their player wheels, it's time to put them to use. Tell your students that all of their hard work has paid off as it is now time to learn how to play the actual Fantasy Baseball game. Let them know that as you introduce the game to them, you will be having them participate in a simulation to help everyone get comfortable with the process the game follows. Explain that you will also be referring to a couple of scoring guides that they will have available to them at all times. These guides contain needed information and will eventually be placed aside as the students get more comfortable with the game.

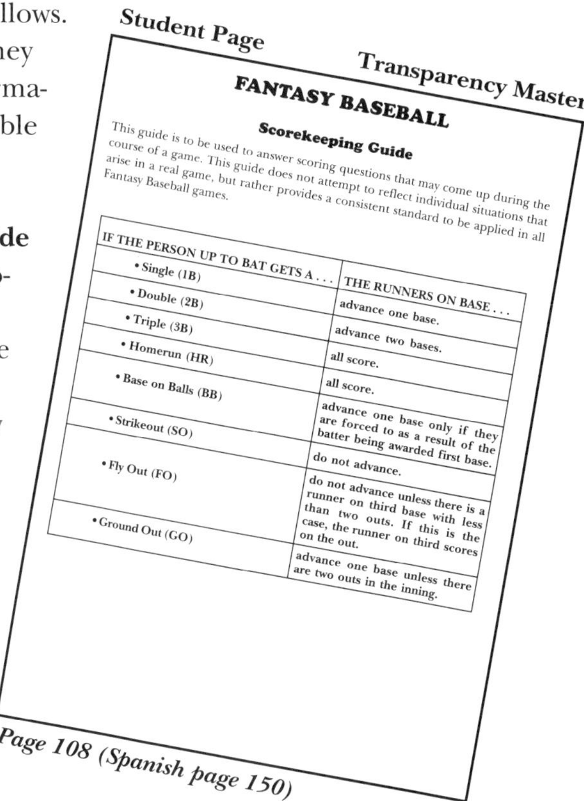

Student Page

Transparency Master

FANTASY BASEBALL

Scorekeeping Guide

This guide is to be used to answer scoring questions that may come up during the course of a game. This guide does not attempt to reflect individual situations that arise in a real game, but rather provides a consistent standard to be applied in all Fantasy Baseball games.

IF THE PERSON UP TO BAT GETS A . . .	THE RUNNERS ON BASE . . .
• Single (1B)	advance one base.
• Double (2B)	advance two bases.
• Triple (3B)	all score.
• Homerun (HR)	all score.
• Base on Balls (BB)	advance one base only if they are forced to as a result of the batter being awarded first base.
• Strikeout (SO)	do not advance.
• Fly Out (FO)	do not advance unless there is a runner on third base with less than two outs. If this is the case, the runner on third scores on the out.
• Ground Out (GO)	advance one base unless there are two outs in the inning.

Page 108 (Spanish page 150)

Pass out a copy of the **Scorekeeping Guide** and the **Pitcher Batting Guide** to each team. Give them a few minutes to look over each guide before proceeding. Walk your students through the **Scorekeeping Guide** explaining that soon they will play and act out a real game. Explain to them that these scorekeeping standards are set to give some equity and consistency to the game because in an actual baseball game, countless factors come into play in every situation:

> ***Where was the ball hit? Did the fielder bobble the ball? How hard was it hit? How fast is the runner? How strong is the fielder's arm?***

Because it would be impossible to consider every variable, this set of common standards has been established. Fantasy Baseball has been designed so that you can play the simulated games by simply referring to the statistics on the backs of the baseball cards.

As you go over this guide, there are a couple of places where you may want to provide some additional explanation.

- If the person up to bat hits a Triple or a Home run, all runners on base score. This means that they go around all of the remaining bases, touch home plate and score a run for their team.

- If the person up to bat receives a Base on Balls, the runners only advance if they are forced to. For example, if there is a runner on first base and a player receives a BB, the runner on first is forced off their base and must advance to second base. If they had been on second base, however, with first base open, they would not have been forced off their base and therefore would not advance.

- If the person up to bat hits a Fly Out with less than two outs and a runner on third base, this runner advances to home and scores a run for their team. All other base runners stay where they're at. This is called a Sacrifice Fly and does not count as an at bat (AB) for the person up to bat. The person up to bat gets credit for an RBI in this situation.

Explain to your students that as you go through the game simulation, they will have an opportunity to ask situational questions that will help them get more comfortable with the game.

Teacher Notes

Although some guidelines have been established for playing the Fantasy Baseball games, nothing should prevent you and your students from making modifications to fit your class needs. Often I have allowed the students to provide input and set up a structure for making changes in the game. This is a unit that uses baseball as a vehicle for investigating the rich math inherent in the game. As long as you continue to explore this richness, altering the game is strongly encouraged.

Student Page Transparency Master

FANTASY BASEBALL

Pitcher Batting Guide

When it is time for your pitcher to bat, you will be using dice as your pitchers do not have player wheels. Below you will find the scoring possibilities for each possible sum of the two dice. Record your pitcher's batting record just the way you would with your other players.

IF YOU ROLL A . . .	YOUR PITCHER GETS A . . .
2	double (2B)
3	single (1B)
4	strikeout (SO)
5	base on balls (BB)
6	fly out (FO)
7	strikeout (SO)
8	ground out (GO)
9	strikeout (SO)
10	fly out (FO)
11	single (1B)
12	homerun (HR)

Page 109 (Spanish page 151)

Have your students refer to the **Pitcher Batting Guide**. Explain that pitchers will be used in the games and that because their batting statistics are not available on the baseball cards, a set of standards have been set for this game.

Explain to your students that these are the guidelines they will need to follow while they are playing the game. Tell them that they will take a closer look at this guide once they have had the opportunity to experience the class simulation and play a practice game against another team.

Game Simulation/Scorekeeping

Let your students know that you are going to lead them through five (5) innings of a simulated game. During this simulation they will get a first hand look at what happens to the runners as each player bats, along with some instruction on how to keep score. Explain to them that as you proceed through the simulation, it will be good for them to ask questions that arise.

Place the transparency of a blank **Scoresheet** on your overhead projector. Ask for a team to volunteer their eight (8) player wheels for use during this simulation. You will need a player for each position, along with the name of one of the team's pitchers.

Student Page Transparency Master

VS AT SCORER DATE

Score by Inning 1 2 3 4 5 6 7 8 9 10 Final Score

Name Pos 1 2 3 4 5 6 7 8 9 10 AB R H 2B 3B HR BB SO RBI

Team Totals

Page 110 (Spanish page 152)

Write the name of the players in random order, in the spaces allocated on the scoresheet. Place the pitcher's name last (as is traditionally done), then ask your students:

Does it really make any difference what order I place these players?

Give them a chance to voice their opinions, then let them know that you will use the recorded order for the simulation and discuss this question further, later on.

Select nine students from the class to represent each of the nine players on the scoresheet. Point out that you are only going to run five innings with this one team and that in a real game, both teams bat each of the nine innings. As each player comes to bat, have the student representing that player come to the front of the classroom. After spinning the wheel, have the student representing the player act out what should happen. For example, a player that gets out can simply return to their seat while a player that gets a hit or base on balls can proceed to the appropriate base. Players should stay on base and move according to the results of the wheels until they either score a run or three outs are recorded to end the inning.

As students act out the results of the wheel spins, point out how to keep score on the **Scoresheet** transparency. The **Sample Scoresheet** that the students will discuss next shows a pretty common set of scorekeeping abbreviations that you can use, including using a K to indicate a strikeout, drawing a slash after the box of the player who makes the last out in an inning, darkening in a diamond when a run is scored to make it easier to tally the total number of runs, indicating RBI's and SF's in the box when the player is at bat, and numbering each out that is made in an inning.

Analyzing a Sample Scoresheet

Now that your students have had the opportunity to watch you model how to keep score of a game, it's an appropriate time to have them analyze a completed scoresheet of a simulated game. Pass out a copy of the **Sample Scoresheet** to each student. Tell your students that their job is to figure out what occurred during each inning of the sample game shown on this sheet. Let them know that you will be asking questions related to the scoresheet in about 10–15 minutes.

Student Page

Transparency Master

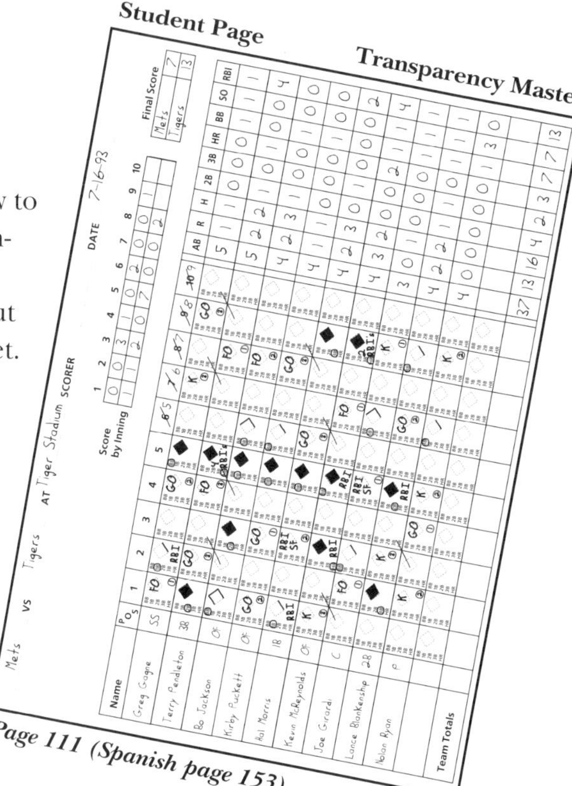

Page 111 (Spanish page 153)

Have your students work in their small groups of 3–4 students to do a play-by-play of the game. Tell them that they can pretend that they are the local announcer who is recalling the game. Encourage them to work together and ask each other questions about the scoresheet as they examine it. Each student should have as their goal, the understanding to answer any question that is asked of them pertaining to this sample scoresheet. Tell them to refer to their **Scoring Guide** and **Pitcher Batting Guide** to help them answer the questions that arise.

After your students have had 10–15 minutes to work with the scoresheeet, have them direct their attention back to you. Following are a few sample questions you can ask of your students while they refer to the scoresheet. You may want to create others or have your students create questions they can ask of each other.

- ***In the 1st inning, what base was Terry Pendleton on before Kirby Puckett grounded out?***

- ***In the 3rd inning, why did Hal Morris get credit for a run batted in?***

- ***In the 5th inning, where were the base runners when Kevin McReynolds came up to bat?***

- ***How many times did Joe Girardi actually come to the plate to bat? Why does he only have 3 AB's in the end-of-game totals?***

Now that you have gone through a game simulation and had your students analyze a sample scoresheet, tell them that it's time for them to play a practice game. Have them pair up with another team in the class and wait for a couple of last-minute instructions prior to starting their own game.

Playing a Practice Game

Once your students have paired up with another team, you will need to be certain that the following instructions are clear to your students before having them play. I suggest going over these before passing out a blank scoresheet to each team.

Teacher Notes

My class decided to address some of the issues that come up during a game by creating their own individual "home team ground rules." These rules (maximum of 3) are followed when a visiting team plays in their "ballpark." Some of the rules revolve around what to do on liners and what happens in the event of a tie game. One team had a rule that allowed for one player to bat twice in the lineup, for himself and as a designated hitter for the pitcher. My students really enjoyed being able to add their ideas to the game.

1. It is possible that when spinning a player wheel, the line on the base of the wheel will end up directly on a line between two statistics. It is crucial that an agreement be made between the two teams playing a game prior to starting. Two options that seem to work are either to spin over or take the better of the two statistics. Any decision is acceptable as long as it is agreed upon by all managers prior to the beginning of the game.

2. It is possible that a game will end in a tie after nine innings. If this happens and time allows, students should get additional scoresheets and continue until one team wins. Remember, the home team (last team to bat) must get their final at bats in order for the game to be official.

3. It is also possible that because of a shortage of time, a game will not go the full nine innings. An official game is one that goes a minimum of five (5) complete innings. If a game has not gone at least five innings, it can be dismissed or completed on the following day.

4. It is important that all managers are involved in the game at all times. The following should be standard practice after the managers have decided on a lineup and the game is ready to begin.

   - Stagger the seating so that you have managers of each team sitting next to each other. Each manager will have a job for their team as well as watching their opposing manager to make sure they do their job correctly.

   - Designate one manager to spin the wheels for the game. The other manager will be responsible for keeping score for the other team when they are up to bat. These roles should alternate from game to game.

   - Tell managers to watch each other closely. You want them to be competitive, yet fair. They should watch closely to catch mistakes and address questions when they come up.

Teacher Notes

During this time, I wander around the classroom, watching the dynamics of the games and looking for any potential trouble situations. I often get a number of questions that can be answered by referring to the *Scorekeeping Guide* or *Sample Scoresheet*. I try to send the students back to these resources to answer their own questions as often as possible. I want them to develop the ability to use what's available so that I'm a minor part of the classroom when they are involved in the game.

After making these points clear to your students, pass out a blank scoresheet to each team and let them play a practice game. They can determine which is the home team (first in the field, last to bat) by flipping a coin or rolling a die. If you happen to have an odd number of teams, tell the odd team out to go ahead and play a game against themselves. The managers will just have to share the wheels and assume the roles of spinner and scorekeeper.

Totaling End of Game Statistics

Once your students have completed their practice games, they will need to total the statistics for each player. You will want to point out the example on the **Sample Scoresheet** before students proceed with their players' stats. There are two (2) key points that students must be clear on to avoid any mistakes while totaling their players' statistics.

1. Bases on balls (BB) and sacrifice flies (SF) do not count as at-bats (AB). Every other time a player has been up to bat should be counted as an at-bat.

2. Hits (H) include the total number of singles (1B), doubles (2B), triples (3B) and home runs (HR) that a player received.

Once your students have totaled each player's statistics, have them complete a team total for the game. For fun, have them calculate their team's batting average, on-base percentage, HR:AB ratio and SO:AB ratio for the game. Give them a chance to compare their results with other teams in the classroom.

Let your students know that it will be very important for them to total each player's statistics at the end of every game they play. By doing this regularly, it will be much easier for them to calculate and record multi-game totals in later activities. Explain to them that not only will they be maintaining their players' statistics for themselves, they will also be using them to determine **League Leaders** in each statistical category.

Teacher Notes

I have found it to work well if I assign students to complete the end of game totals for homework. I keep a check-off sheet on a clipboard and managers must show me their completed scoresheets the following day before they are allowed to play their next game. During the regular season, they forfeit the game if they are not prepared to play. This seems to motivate most students to keep on top of tabulating their end of game totals.

Investigating the Pitcher Batting Guide

You mentioned to your students that they would be returning to the **Pitcher Batting Guide** that was presented to them earlier. Now is a good time to have them take a close look and investigate the mathematical implications of these guidelines. This type of investigation is best led through a series of questions, then letting the students discuss and argue their reasoning. During this investigation, your goal is to have them look beyond the obvious to complete a more thorough analysis of this guide.

Have your students take a look at the chart that determines what a pitcher will do at bat with the roll of two dice. Ask them to consider the following questions:

> ***What is the ratio of chances of getting a hit to possible outcomes? What percentage of possible outcomes is this?***
>
> ***What is the ratio of chances of reaching base to possible outcomes? What percentage of possible outcomes is this?***
>
> ***What is the ratio of chances of getting out to possible outcomes?***

Transparency Master

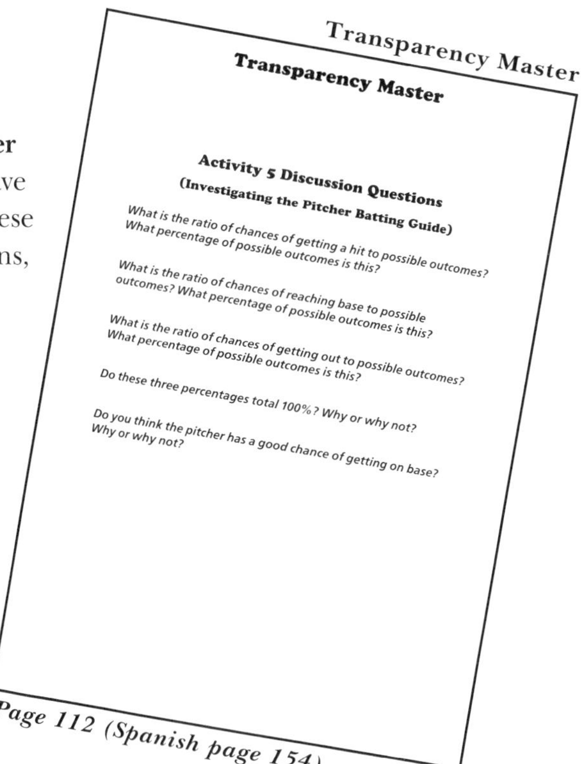

Transparency Master

Activity 5 Discussion Questions
(Investigating the Pitcher Batting Guide)

What is the ratio of chances of getting a hit to possible outcomes? What percentage of possible outcomes is this?

What is the ratio of chances of reaching base to possible outcomes? What percentage of possible outcomes is this?

What is the ratio of chances of getting out to possible outcomes? What percentage of possible outcomes is this?

Do these three percentages total 100%? Why or why not?

Do you think the pitcher has a good chance of getting on base? Why or why not?

Page 112 (Spanish page 154)

What percentage of possible outcomes is this?

Do these three percentages total 100%? Why or why not?

Do you think the pitcher has a good chance of getting on base? Why or why not?

Allow your students some time to play around with these questions. Encourage them to compare their results with others sitting at their tables. Many of your students will initially look at there being 11 possible outcomes and work up ratios and percentages of 4:11 or 36%, 5:11 or 45% and 6:11 or 55%. Some will wonder why they don't total 100% until someone points out that the ratio of hits : possible outcomes is included in the ratio of reaching base : possible outcomes. Based on this information, they may conclude that the pitcher has a pretty good chance of reaching base.

Teacher Notes

Some of my students had difficulty in seeing that 2 + 3 was a different outcome than 3 + 2. To make this clearer, I had them use 1 red die and 1 white die. Using these, I was able to point out the difference between *combinations* and *permutations.* Once they could see this, they had no trouble finding all of the possible outcomes for sums with two dice.

If none of your students shows any further insight into these questions, ask them the following:

How many different ways can you roll a sum of two with 2 dice? What about a sum of three? Four? Five? etc. Will this have any effect on the ratios you just figured?

Have your students start listing the possible outcomes for rolling a pair of dice.

Pitchers' Hitting Possibilities

	1	2	3	4	5	6
1	2B	1B	SO	BB	FO	SO
2	1B	SO	BB	FO	SO	GO
3	SO	BB	FO	SO	GO	SO
4	BB	FO	SO	GO	SO	FO
5	FO	SO	GO	SO	FO	1B
6	SO	GO	SO	FO	1B	HR

If your students are having difficulty organizing the possible outcomes, you may want to suggest that they construct a matrix as an organizational tool.

As they start filling in the chart, they'll begin to see that the probability for getting a hit or reaching base decreases from their original figure while the probability for making an out increases.

Refer them back to the same questions you asked previously. You will find that they now present ratios and percentages like 6:36 or 17%, 10:36 or 28%, and 26:36 or 72%.

After considering all possibilities, your students may present a different answer to the last question you presented to them. Point out that things aren't always what they seem — that in this case, the probability of the pitcher getting a hit or reaching base safely is not as good as it first appeared.

You might want to conclude this investigation by pointing out to your students that using this pitcher guide is one of the rules of the game. You might want to ask them if they think this is a good part of the game or if they think it should be different. If you find that they don't particularly like this part, you might suggest that as a class, you look at ways of altering this guide. You can mention that rules of games are constantly being tinkered with to make a game exciting. This tinkering with rules also goes on in real baseball — shorter fences, designated hitters, beefed-up baseballs, etc., have all been added to the game to make it more exciting and keep the games close.

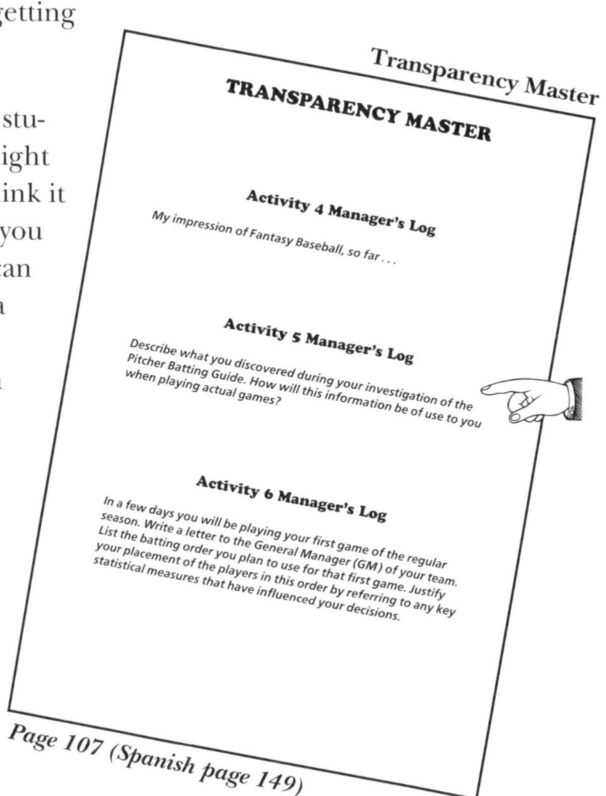
Transparency Master

TRANSPARENCY MASTER

Activity 4 Manager's Log

My impression of Fantasy Baseball, so far . . .

Activity 5 Manager's Log

Describe what you discovered during your investigation of the Pitcher Batting Guide. How will this information be of use to you when playing actual games?

Activity 6 Manager's Log

In a few days you will be playing your first game of the regular season. Write a letter to the General Manager (GM) of your team. List the batting order you plan to use for that first game. Justify your placement of the players in this order by referring to any key statistical measures that have influenced your decisions.

Page 107 (Spanish page 149)

Activity Wrap — Practice Game/Manager's Log

If time allows, let your students play another practice game against a different team in the class. Again, stress the importance of every manager being involved in the game and helping others to improve their scorekeeping skills.

Have students take out their Manager's Log. Write the following on the chalkboard or overhead:

> ***Describe what you discovered during your investigation of the Pitcher Batting Guide. How will this information be of use to you when playing actual games?***

Provide your students with 10–15 minutes of "quiet time" to complete this entry in their log. If time allows, have them share their writing in small groups and possibly call on a few interested students to share with the class.

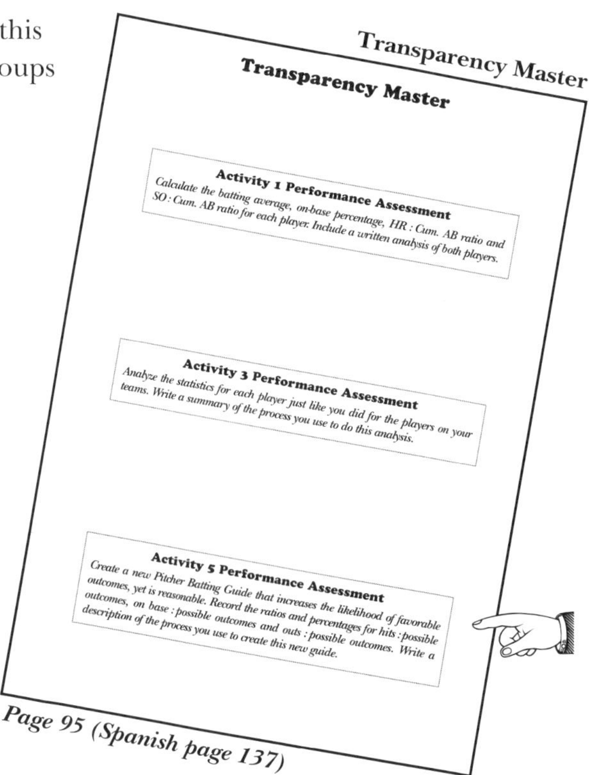
Transparency Master

Transparency Master

Activity 1 Performance Assessment
Calculate the batting average, on-base percentage, HR : Cum. AB ratio and SO : Cum. AB ratio for each player. Include a written analysis of both players.

Activity 3 Performance Assessment
Analyze the statistics for each player just like you did for the players on your teams. Write a summary of the process you use to do this analysis.

Activity 5 Performance Assessment
Create a new Pitcher Batting Guide that increases the likelihood of favorable outcomes, yet is reasonable. Record the ratios and percentages for hits : possible outcomes, on base : possible outcomes and outs : possible outcomes. Write a description of the process you use to create this new guide.

Page 95 (Spanish page 137)

Performance Assessment

Have students create a new* Pitcher Batting Guide *that increases the likelihood of favorable outcomes, yet is reasonable. Have them record the ratios and percentages for hits : possible outcomes, on base : possible outcomes and outs : possible outcomes. Included with this data should be a written description of the process they used to create this new guide.

Looking Ahead

Tell your students that they are about to enter into a 5-game exhibition season. This will give them an opportunity to sharpen their scorekeeping skills as well as experiment with different lineups. Inform them that they will be looking at strategies for player placement in their lineups to increase their likelihood of scoring more runs.

ACTIVITY 6
EXHIBITION GAMES/SEASON SCHEDULE

◆ ◆ ◆

Summary

Students participate in a 5-game exhibition season. This provides them with practice scorekeeping, allows them to experiment with different lineups and get comfortable with compiling player statistics. They also explore the purpose of player placement in the batting order and look at a new statistic, slugging percentage. Finally, students are given the task of creating a regular season schedule for the teams in their class.

Math Content

- collecting, organizing, interpreting and analyzing data
- fraction/decimal/percentage equivalency
- deriving and analyzing formulas
- determining counting arrangements of discrete objects

Classroom Time

4–5 days

Materials

Student Pages:

- **Challenge Problem #2: Flashy Uniforms** (1 per student)
- **Team Stat Sheet** (1 per team)
- **Sample Schedules** (1 per student)
- **Assignment — Regular Season Schedule** (1 per student)

Transparencies:

- **Sample Schedules**
- **Activity 6 Discussion Questions (Player Placement — Does It Really Matter?)**
- **Activity 6 Discussion Questions (A Return to Looking at Player Placement)**
- **Activity 6 Performance Assessment**

Activity 6 Manager's Log Transparency
Scoresheets (blank)
Player wheels
Calculators
Paper and pencils
Manager's Log (journal)

Pre-Activity Preparation

Run off enough blank scoresheets so that each team has access to 6–8 of them.

Challenge Problem #2: Flashy Uniforms

Before you have your students begin their exhibition season, present each of them with a copy of **Challenge Problem #2**. This problem involves distinguishing between combinations and permutations, systematically organizing data and applying the basic counting principle. It also allows students to express their artistic abilities by designing an outrageous team uniform for display.

Read through the problem with your students and give them a little time to ask any questions they need to clarify the problem. Try to refrain from giving too much information but rather ask questions that will help students to answer their own questions. At the end of this activity you can find some sample questions that you can ask them at this point, over the course of the week as your students work on the problem, or when you decide to process the problem. Direct your students to use the **Problem of the Week (P.O.W.)** procedure that was presented to them with **Challenge Problem #1**. Explain that they are to work on this problem on their own time and that as a class, they will look at what they have done at the end of this activity.

Teacher Notes

My students had many different approaches to this problem. Some started making combinations without any organized plan while others made organized lists or constructed tree diagrams. Many initially failed to distinguish between permutations (arrangements of objects in a particular order) and combinations (arrangements of objects without regard to order) until I referred them back to the *Pitcher Batting Guide* investigation. From here they were able to apply their understanding to find the different color variations for each article of clothing, then apply the Basic Counting Principle to determine the number of uniform combinations.

Playing Exhibition Games

Your students need time to play a few practice games without any instruction or interruptions. Set aside the first 2 ½ days of this activity solely for this purpose. Allow the students to choose the teams they want to play as long as they play against five different teams. Allow them to play two games the first day, then insist that they show you their completed end-of-game totals prior to playing any games the following day. You will want to get your students into the habit of completing these totals so that as the regular season progresses, they are used to keeping a running compilation of their players' statistics.

By the middle of the third day of this activity, your students should be finishing the fifth and final game of this exhibition season. Once they have completed this final game, instruct them to total each player's statistics for the five games and enter their totals on a blank **Team Stat Sheet**. At this point, have them fill in all of the columns except for SLG. %. (They will be learning about slugging percentage later in this activity.) They may need to refer back to their notes for calculating AVG. and On-base % to calculate these statistical measures for each of their players.

Student Page

Name ____________

Date ____________

Period ____

CHALLENGE PROBLEM #2

Flashy Uniforms

To promote attendance at your team's upcoming games, you have decided to furnish your players with outlandish uniforms. You believe that the flashier the uniforms, the greater the fan interest. The problem is, how will you decide on which color combination to use for your new uniforms?

You know that you need to purchase the following articles for your players:

jersey, pants, stirrups, shoes and a **hat.**

The following colors are available for your uniforms:

black, white, peach, teal, red, blue and **orange.**

In order to stay within league guidelines, you must adhere to the following:

- Your jerseys must consist of **three** different colors
- Your pants must consist of **two** different colors
- Your stirrups must be **one** solid color
- Your shoes must consist of **two** different colors with the laces being of a different color than those of the shoes
- Your hat must consist of **three** different colors

How many different color combinations are possible for a complete uniform if you follow the league guidelines stated above?

** Design and draw a uniform for your team using one of the possible combinations.

Page 113 (Spanish page 155)

Player Placement — Does It Really Matter?

When your students have finished playing their exhibition games, present the following question to your students and give them an opportunity to share their responses in small groups and with the whole class.

Does it really matter what order you place your players in the batting lineup?

Student Page

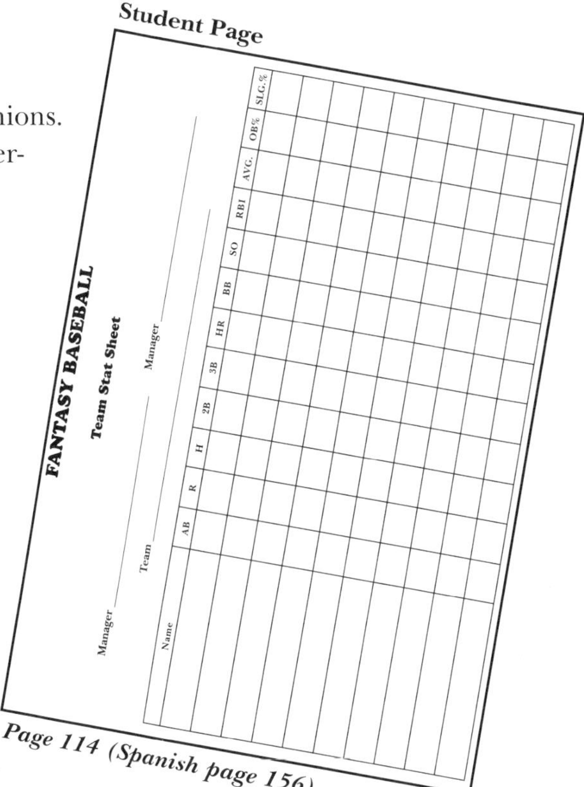
FANTASY BASEBALL
Team Stat Sheet

Manager ______ Manager ______ Team ______

Name	AB	R	H	2B	3B	HR	BB	SO	RBI	AVG.	OB%	SLG.%

Page 114 (Spanish page 156)

Encourage them to explain their reasoning when presenting their opinions. You might want to keep notes on a large sheet of butcher paper or the overhead so that students have a visual reminder of what has been said.

Have your students refer to their completed **Team Stat Sheet** showing their players' statistics from the 5-game exhibition season. Read the brief paragraph written below out loud to the class:

> ***Managers need to make decisions every day regarding what order they will place their players in the lineup. The order they choose is often an attempt to make the most of each player's abilities. The goal of the manager is to have his/her team score as many runs as possible during the course of a game. Consider the following questions as you look at the results of your 5-game exhibition season. Remember, there are no right or wrong ways to order the players in your lineup, however, carefully planning your order can increase the probability of scoring more runs.***

Present your students with the following questions to consider when making up their lineup. You may want to write them on the chalkboard, use the transparency on the overhead, or present them orally, one at a time. These are not questions for the students to answer on a sheet of paper and turn in but rather questions they'll want to consider and discuss with their co-manager. You can either have your students discuss them as co-managers, in small groups or as a whole class. Regardless of the process you use, your students may want to record responses to some of the questions as this information could be useful to them in the upcoming season.

Following each set of questions is information that might be useful to you, the teacher. As you walk around the classroom listening to the students or facilitate a whole class discussion, these notes may help you redirect some of the discussions to get students to look critically at the placement of the players in their lineups.

- ***Look at your Team Stat Sheet. Do all of your players have the same number of at bats? Which players tend to have more, those that are placed at the beginning of the lineup or those placed at the end? Is there a significant difference? According to their statistics, are there certain players you would want to have bat more than others?***

  (It is most likely that some players have more at-bats than others. Players at the front of the lineup often get an extra at-bat during the course of a game. Over the course of a 50 game season, this could mean an additional 50 at-bats. A team would benefit most by having the players that reach base more often getting these extra at-bats.)

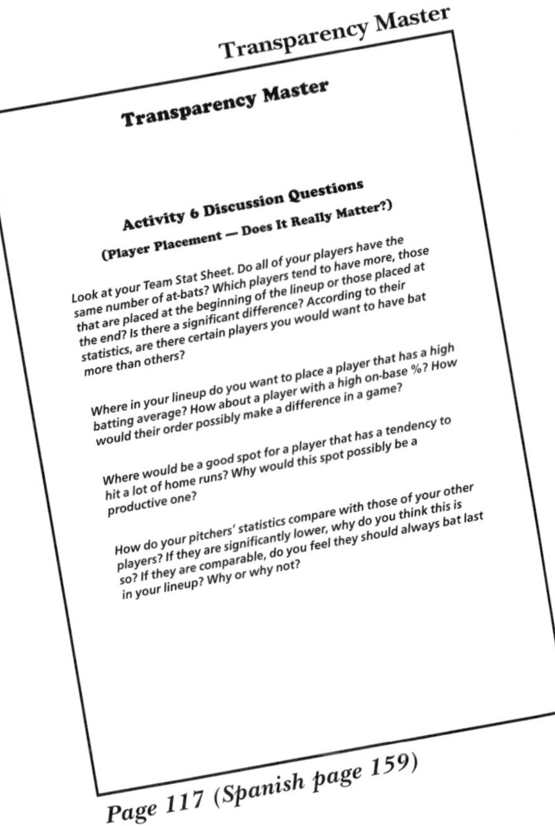

Transparency Master

Activity 6 Discussion Questions

(Player Placement — Does It Really Matter?)

Look at your Team Stat Sheet. Do all of your players have the same number of at-bats? Which players tend to have more, those that are placed at the beginning of the lineup or those placed at the end? Is there a significant difference? According to their statistics, are there certain players you would want to have bat more than others?

Where in your lineup do you want to place a player that has a high batting average? How about a player with a high on-base %? How would their order possibly make a difference in a game?

Where would be a good spot for a player that has a tendency to hit a lot of home runs? Why would this spot possibly be a productive one?

How do your pitchers' statistics compare with those of your other players? If they are significantly lower, why do you think this is so? If they are comparable, do you feel they should always bat last in your lineup? Why or why not?

Transparency Master

Page 117 (Spanish page 159)

- ***Where in your lineup do you want to place a player that has a high batting average? How about a player with a high on-base %? How would their order possibly make a difference in a game?***

  (Players of this caliber are often placed at the beginning of the line-up. If they have a strong success rate for reaching base, you want them to get up to bat as many times as possible during a game. The more they are on base, the better the chance that one of your sluggers will knock them in (score a run). The more runs you score, the better chance of winning the game.)

- ***Where would be a good spot for a player that has a tendency to hit a lot of home runs? Why would this spot possibly be a productive one?***

  (Home run hitters are often placed in the 4 and 5 positions in the line-up. Once again, if there are runners on base when they come up to bat, there is a better chance that more runs will be scored.)

- ***How do your pitchers' statistics compare with those of your other players? If they are significantly lower, why do you think this is so? If they are comparable, do you feel they should always bat last in your lineup? Why or why not?***

  (Although it is likely that the pitchers on each team do fall at the bottom of each statistical category, it is possible that this is not the case. This question leads to some great discussion about what the mathematical likelihood is and what the actual statistics for the 5 games show.)

A New Statistic — Slugging Percentage

Ask your students to think about the following situation:

> ***You are batting in the last of the 9th inning. Your team is two runs down but you're starting to put together a rally. You have runners on second and third with two outs. What player on your team do you want coming up to bat in this situation? Explain why you want this particular player.***

Give your students an opportunity to share their responses. You will find that most will want a player that has a strong chance of getting a game-winning home run or at the very least, a game-tieing double. When they share, push your students to explain how they came up with the player they did. Ask them to mention any statistical data they referred to when making their decisions.

Have your students work together as pairs or in groups of four to create a method or methods for comparing players that hit for power. Tell them to refer back to their players' statistics on the baseball cards and draw their comparisons using fractions, decimals or percentages. You might suggest that they also refer to their players' **Player Analysis Charts** for additional ideas on how to draw these comparisons.

Teacher Notes

It was interesting to see the variety of methods my students used to compare power hitters. Some just found totals of extra base hits (doubles, triples, HR's) while others took it a step further and found ratios of extra base hits/at bats. Some even converted these ratios to their decimal equivalent and compared players by referring to percentages. Having them share their different methods was extremely enlightening — after some discussion, my students decided that it would be nice if there was a uniform way of making these comparisons. This was exactly what I was hoping they would come to understand!

After your students have had a chance to share their methods of comparison, mention that baseball analysts have created another statistic that provides managers with additional information about a player's offensive capabilities. This statistical measure is called the Slugging Percentage or Slugging Average. This percentage or average is used by managers to determine whether or not a player hits with any power - in other words, do they frequently get hits that take them past first base. By looking at a player's Slugging Percentage, managers are able to determine whether or not a particular player is better suited for a batting position where there's a greater probability of having runners on base. This is important in the strategy of the game because having runners on base increases the probability of the batter getting a higher number of runs batted in (RBI's).

Explain to your students that some time ago, baseball analysts created their own formula for calculating this statistic. Present your students with the following formula:

$$\frac{\textbf{\# of total bases from hits}}{\textbf{at bats (AB)}} = \textbf{Slugging Percentage}$$

Ask your students to think about **how** they could find the number of total bases from hits that a player accumulated. Once again, allow them to share the different methods they create. If no one presents the following equation, you can present it to your students as another method:

$$[H - (2B + 3B + HR) + 2(2B) + 3(3B) + 4(HR)]$$

Ask your students:

> ***In this equation, why do you need to subtract the number of doubles, triples and home runs from the number of hits?***

You want your students to see that they must first determine how many of the player's hits were singles before calculating the remainder of the total bases.

Do a few examples of calculating this statistic on the overhead or chalkboard. The Slugging Percentage or Slugging Average is written to three decimal places (ie. .463). As with on-base percentage, this statistic is commonly displayed as a decimal instead of a percentage. You might also mention that, as with batting average and on-base percentage, this statistic is also recorded to three decimal places for precision sake.

Once your students can confidently perform this calculation, have them figure the Slugging Percentage (SLG.) for the five exhibition games for each of their players. After completing the statistics for each player, instruct your students to complete their Team Totals at the bottom of the **Team Stat Sheet**. Tell them that they will want to have this completed **Team Stat Sheet** available before considering some additional questions regarding placement of their players in the batting order.

A Return To Looking At Player Placement

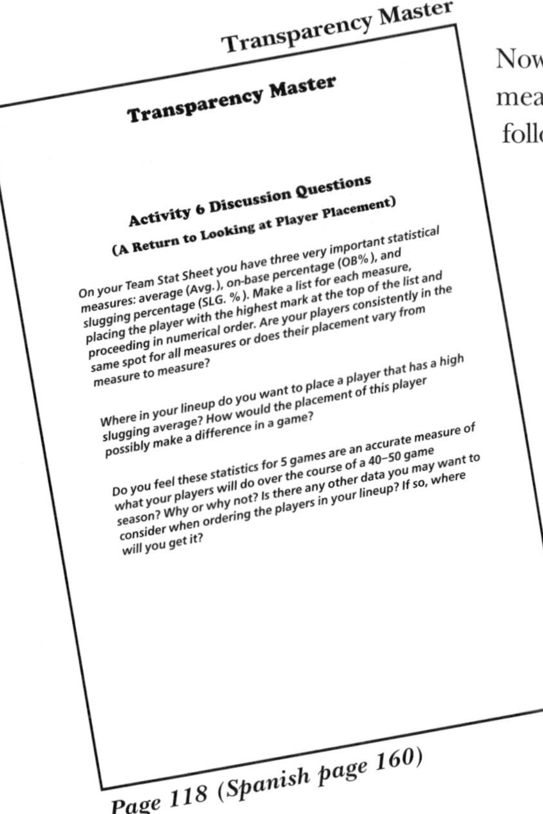

Transparency Master

Transparency Master

Activity 6 Discussion Questions

(A Return to Looking at Player Placement)

On your Team Stat Sheet you have three very important statistical measures: average (Avg.), on-base percentage (OB%), and slugging percentage (SLG. %). Make a list for each measure, placing the player with the highest mark at the top of the list and proceeding in numerical order. Are your players consistently in the same spot for all measures or does their placement vary from measure to measure?

Where in your lineup do you want to place a player that has a high slugging average? How would the placement of this player possibly make a difference in a game?

Do you feel these statistics for 5 games are an accurate measure of what your players will do over the course of a 40–50 game season? Why or why not? Is there any other data you may want to consider when ordering the players in your lineup? If so, where will you get it?

Page 118 (Spanish page 160)

Now that your students have had the opportunity to investigate another statistical measure, let them continue their discussions on player placement. Once again, following each set of questions is information to help you facilitate student discussion.

- ***On your Team Stat Sheet you have three very important statistical measures: average (AVG.), On-base percentage (OB%), and slugging percentage (Slg. %). Make a list for each measure, placing the player with the highest mark at the top of the list and proceeding in numerical order. Are your players consistently in the same spot for all measures or does their placement vary from measure to measure?***

  (Although it is possible to have a player be consistent across the board in all three categories, it is unlikely. Players with a high AVG. often have a high On-base % as well. Your students may find that the players with a high Slugging Average are those that are 4th or 5th in the other categories.)

- ***Where in your lineup do you want to place a player that has a high slugging average? How would the placement of this player possibly make a difference in a game?***

  (Some good spots for your sluggers are the 3, 4, 5 and 6 positions in the lineup. You want them to follow players that don't hit for power yet have a high probability of getting on base. The more runners on base when a slugger comes to bat, the better the chance that your team will score more runs.)

- ***Do you feel these statistics for 5 games are an accurate measure of what your players will do over the course of a 40–50 game season? Why or why not? Is there any other data you may want to consider when ordering the players in your lineup? If so, where will you get it?***

  (Although some students may feel like the statistics for the 5 games are an accurate measure, in most cases they are not. They would need a considerable amount of generated data to truly get an accurate measure of what their players will do over the course of the regular season and even this would not necessarily be accurate. Another source for lineup placement would be the Player Analysis Charts they completed prior to making the player wheels. This actually provides a better frame of reference for a 40–50 game season.)

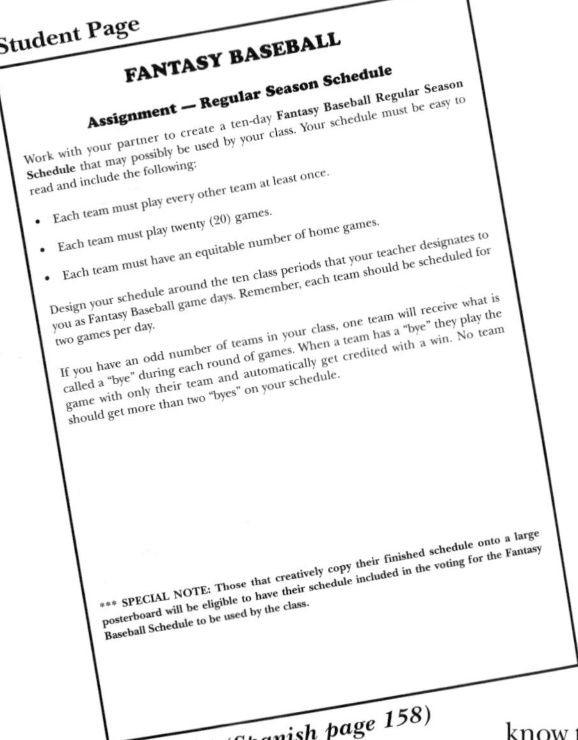

Student Page

FANTASY BASEBALL

Assignment — Regular Season Schedule

Work with your partner to create a ten-day **Fantasy Baseball Regular Season Schedule** that may possibly be used by your class. Your schedule must be easy to read and include the following:

- Each team must play every other team at least once.
- Each team must play twenty (20) games.
- Each team must have an equitable number of home games.

Design your schedule around the ten class periods that your teacher designates to you as Fantasy Baseball game days. Remember, each team should be scheduled for two games per day.

If you have an odd number of teams in your class, one team will receive what is called a "bye" during each round of games. When a team has a "bye" they play the game with only their team and automatically get credited with a win. No team should get more than two "byes" on your schedule.

***** SPECIAL NOTE: Those that creatively copy their finished schedule onto a large posterboard will be eligible to have their schedule included in the voting for the Fantasy Baseball Schedule to be used by the class.**

Page 116 (Spanish page 158)

Tell your students that the purpose of looking at these questions was to get them to focus on the multitude of possibilities for the order of their lineups. Explain that there is no such thing as a right or wrong lineup but that by looking at available data, they'll be prepared to make decisions that increase the probability of their team scoring more runs. Let them know that they will be referring back to what they have done here during the next entry in their Manager's Log.

Assignment — Regular Season Schedule

Let your students know that following the next activity, they will be starting the regular season of Fantasy Baseball. In order to get the season underway, however, you will need to have a schedule that shows which teams play which during the initial 10-day season. Tell your students that this is a task that you are going to present to them to do outside of class. Explain that it will be due at the end of Activity 7 and that the class will vote on which student-created schedule they will use for their regular season.

Recording on a large sheet of chart paper, chalkboard or the overhead, lead your students in a short brainstorming session related to creating a schedule. Ask students to present their ideas (strategies) for creating a 20-game schedule for all of the teams in the class. Point out that when scheduling, the home team is usually listed second. Their schedule should allow each team to be the home team for an equitable number of times.

If none of your students suggests the strategy of breaking this task down to a smaller one, you might want to suggest this to them. The following task involves creating a schedule on a much smaller scale and will give your students some baseline experiences to draw from.

> ***Let's take a look at creating a possible schedule for 3 days if we had 8 teams in the class. Each team needs to be scheduled to play 2 games per day and shouldn't play the same team more than once.***
>
> ***Here are the teams that we will use for our sample schedule:***

Yankees	*Padres*
Tigers	*Giants*
Angels	*Phillies*
Orioles	*Mets*

> ***The days we will use are Monday, Tuesday and Wednesday. What are some possibilities for a schedule on Monday? Remember, each team is to play 2 games.***

Allow your students to play around with the different combinations that can be created with these 8 teams. You may want to have them find all of the possible combinations, then create their schedule from this data. Your students will have different strategies for scheduling the teams — some will have teams play the teams in the other league first, some will alternate from league to league and others will seem to have no order at all. Some students will use the team names while others will assign numbers or letters to represent a team. Encourage students to use a method that they are comfortable with and to be prepared to share their method with others in the class.

Give students a chance to share their schedules in small groups and possibly with the class. Some **Sample Schedules** are also provided as a Student

Teacher Notes

Is Padres vs. Tigers the same as Tigers vs. Padres? This was a question that was asked in one of my classes. It was quite interesting to listen to my students reason through this question and try to convince each other that *they* were correct. This question provided another opportunity to reinforce the similarities and differences with *combinations* and *permutations.*

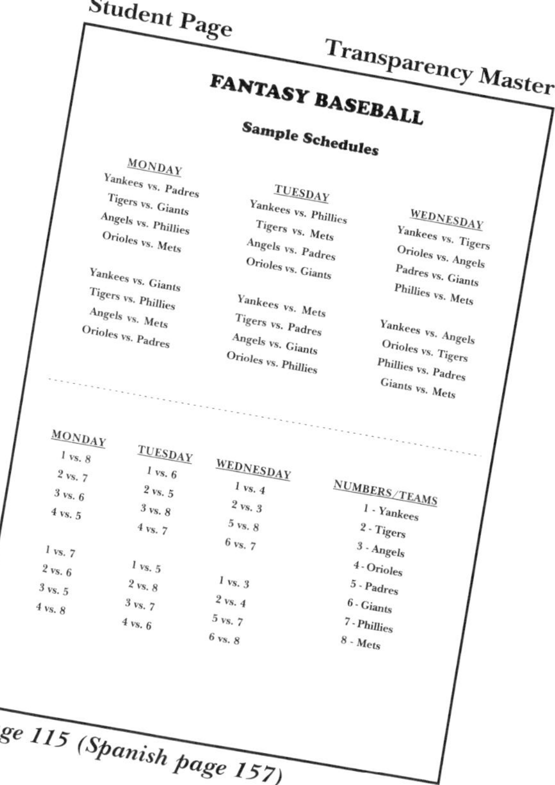
Student Page — Transparency Master

FANTASY BASEBALL

Sample Schedules

MONDAY	TUESDAY	WEDNESDAY
Yankees vs. Padres	Yankees vs. Phillies	Yankees vs. Tigers
Tigers vs. Giants	Tigers vs. Mets	Orioles vs. Angels
Angels vs. Phillies	Angels vs. Padres	Padres vs. Giants
Orioles vs. Mets	Orioles vs. Giants	Phillies vs. Mets
Yankees vs. Giants	Yankees vs. Mets	Yankees vs. Angels
Tigers vs. Phillies	Tigers vs. Padres	Orioles vs. Tigers
Angels vs. Mets	Angels vs. Giants	Phillies vs. Padres
Orioles vs. Padres	Orioles vs. Phillies	Giants vs. Mets

MONDAY	TUESDAY	WEDNESDAY	NUMBERS/TEAMS
1 vs. 8	1 vs. 6	1 vs. 4	1 - Yankees
2 vs. 7	2 vs. 5	2 vs. 3	2 - Tigers
3 vs. 6	3 vs. 8	5 vs. 8	3 - Angels
4 vs. 5	4 vs. 7	6 vs. 7	4 - Orioles
1 vs. 7	1 vs. 5	1 vs. 3	5 - Padres
2 vs. 6	2 vs. 8	2 vs. 4	6 - Giants
3 vs. 5	3 vs. 7	5 vs. 7	7 - Phillies
4 vs. 8	4 vs. 6	6 vs. 8	8 - Mets

Page 115 (Spanish page 157)

Teacher Notes

What I wanted to see from my students was an organized method for recording the different combinations. I didn't always see effective organization right away but found that students often tried new methods after seeing what others were doing. What I found was useful was having students themselves point out the benefits and drawbacks to their method of organization. By doing this, they had to think through what they were doing and whether or not it made sense. Often during this process, they found ways to increase their efficiency.

Teacher Notes

I also had my students share the new uniforms they created for their teams. This provided them with a visual representation of some of the different combinations that were possible. We decided to create a new bulletin board and display the uniforms. When this happened, those who hadn't drawn a uniform got busy as they wanted theirs included with the rest.

Page and Transparency Master. You may elect to show these sample schedules to the class or work through one with them if they don't appear from student work. Once you've given your students the opportunity to share their abbreviated schedules, pass out the **Regular Season Schedule** assignment sheet and discuss it briefly with the class.

Be sure to let your students know that you expect them to work with their co-managers as a team (as always) and that their schedules are due at the end of Activity 7 (next activity). Let them know that only poster-size schedules will be included in the voting as the selected schedule will be posted in the classroom as the official Fantasy Baseball Regular Season Schedule.

Challenge Problem #2 — Processing the Math

As you conclude this activity, set aside ½ to one whole period for processing **Challenge Problem #2**. During this processing time, allow students to first share their responses in small, cooperative groups. From this sharing, have each group attempt to reach consensus on a solution that seems reasonable to them as well as a process or processes used to get this solution. Facilitate a whole class sharing/discussion with each group briefly summarizing what they have done. The key here is to focus on the multitude of methods used by your students to work towards a reasonable solution for this problem.

The following questions may help you process this Challenge Problem with your students. You may want to present your students with some of these questions as they are grappling with the problem. These questions are not all-inclusive — while working through the problem you may discover others that would be of benefit to your students. Write them down and use them. Try to pull as much mathematics from the problem as you possibly can.

Which items must consist of 3 colors? 2 colors? 1 color?

Look at the first three available colors. When designing a jersey, is black, white and peach the same as peach, white and black? Why or why not?

Using the guidelines stated, which of these articles possesses the largest number of possibilities? Why is this part of the uniform so different from the rest?

How many different possibilities are there for just the jersey and the pants? How did you use the combinations for each item to find the possible combinations for both items?

Can you find a shortcut for figuring the different combinations for the jersey, pants and stirrups? If so, explain your method and why it works. If you have one, how will your shortcut help you solve the rest of the problem?

Is this a good problem? Why or why not?

Activity Wrap — Manager's Log

Have your students take out their Manager's Logs and prepare to write to the following prompt. They may want to have the notes they collected while looking at player statistics for placement in their lineup. Write the following on the overhead or chalkboard:

> ***In a few days you will be playing your first game of the regular season. Write a letter to the General Manager (GM) of your team. List the batting order you plan to use for that first game. Justify your placement of players in this order by referring to any key statistical measures that have influenced your decisions.***

Provide your students with 10–15 minutes of "quiet time" to complete this entry in their logs. If time allows, let students share their responses in small groups and those that are interested, with the whole class.

Transparency Master

TRANSPARENCY MASTER

Activity 4 Manager's Log

My impression of Fantasy Baseball, so far . . .

Activity 5 Manager's Log

Describe what you discovered during your investigation of the Pitcher Batting Guide. How will this information be of use to you when playing actual games?

Activity 6 Manager's Log

In a few days you will be playing your first game of the regular season. Write a letter to the General Manager (GM) of your team. List the batting order you plan to use for that first game. Justify your placement of the players in this order by referring to any key statistical measures that have influenced your decisions.

Page 107 (Spanish page 149)

> ### Performance Assessment
> ***Present students with statistics from the back of two baseball cards (eligible years — 200+ AB's). Have them describe where in their batting order they would place these players, providing statistical data that supports their decisions.***

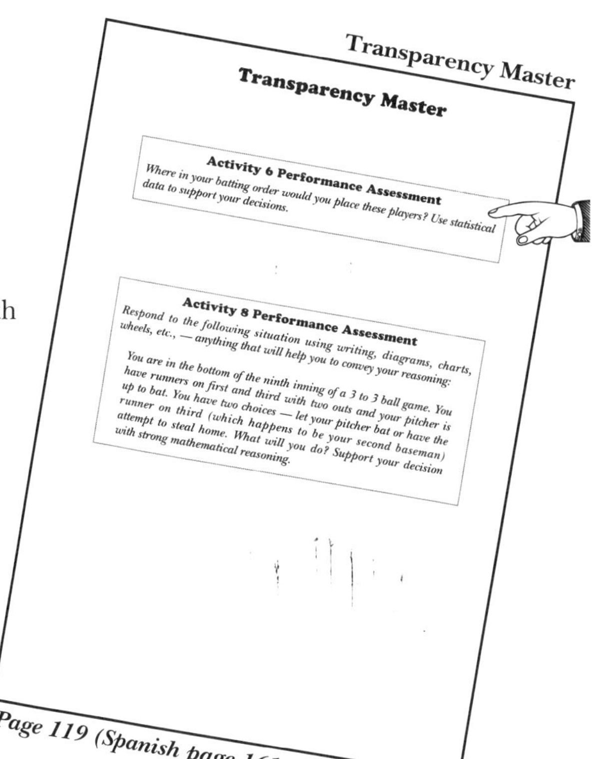
Transparency Master

Transparency Master

Activity 6 Performance Assessment

Where in your batting order would you place these players? Use statistical data to support your decisions.

Activity 8 Performance Assessment

Respond to the following situation using writing, diagrams, charts, wheels, etc., — anything that will help you to convey your reasoning:

You are in the bottom of the ninth inning of a 3 to 3 ball game. You have runners on first and third with two outs and your pitcher is up to bat. You have two choices — let your pitcher bat or have the runner on third (which happens to be your second baseman) attempt to steal home. What will you do? Support your decision with strong mathematical reasoning.

Page 119 (Spanish page 161)

Looking Ahead

Tell your students that during the next few days, they will be exploring the role of probability in Fantasy Baseball by doing some investigative work with their player wheels. Let them know that this will be the last activity before starting the Fantasy Baseball regular season games.

Activity 7
Player Wheel/Probability Connection

◆ ◆ ◆

Summary

Students explore the relationships between their player wheels and the probability of certain outcomes. They run experiments with their wheels and compare the theoretical probability with the experimental probability. After considerable experimentation and discussion, students are asked to record their predictions for what their players' statistics will look like after playing 20 games.

Math Content

- predicting probability of an event
- collecting, organizing, displaying and analyzing data
- constructing circle graphs
- theoretical vs. experimental probability
- predicting outcomes using theoretical and experimental data

Classroom Time

2–3 days

Materials

Student Pages:

  Theoretical vs. Experimental Probability recording sheets (1 per student)

Transparencies:

  Theoretical vs. Experimental Probability recording sheet

  Activity 7 Manager's Log

Player Wheels

Player Analysis Charts (completed)

Team Stat Sheet (1 per student)

Paper and pencils

Calculators

1-cm. graph paper

Colored pencils or markers

Manager's Log

Pre-Activity Preparation

In the course of this activity, your students will be making predictions about what a player's statistics would be after spinning their player wheel 360 times. To help your students understand some difficult concepts in probability related to this activity, I feel it is worthwhile to spend some time experimenting and thinking about the activity prior to presenting it to your students. By doing it yourself, you are able to draw from firsthand experiences as you engage your students in discussions about probability. This makes it easier for you to address questions they may have during the activity.

Using the completed **Player Analysis Chart** from your player wheel example, complete the first section of the **Theoretical vs. Experimental Probability** recording sheet. Then record your prediction for what your player's statistics would look like after 360 spins. Be sure that the total of all categories (excluding FO & GO as these are subsets of Other Outs) is equal to 360 (Cum. AB's).

Keep a tally of 360 spins of your wheel. You may want to run this experiment in three 100-spin increments and a final 60-spin trial. Once you have finished 360 spins, find the totals and record the necessary information on the last section of the chart.

Compare your final results with your prediction. Were you close? Compare your final results with the theoretical probability section of the chart. How do your results and this section compare? Chances are, the experimental probability came closer to reflecting the theoretical probability after 360 spins than it did after 100 spins. What do you think would happen if you spun your wheel 360 more times?

Probability Experiment — 100 Spins

Explain to your students that during the course of the next two to three days, they will be learning some things about probability and how it relates to the player wheels they have constructed. Tell your students that to begin with, you would like them to choose only one of their players — the one they feel is the best player they have — and work with that player wheel for the duration of this activity. This will help them keep a focus on the concepts you will be introducing.

On a blank sheet of paper, have the students make a tally sheet that includes each of the possible outcomes on the player wheel.

1B 2B 3B HR BB SO FO GO

Tell your students that they should work together with their co-manager throughout this activity. Ask them to spin the wheel they've selected 10 times and tally the results. Looking at the data they've collected, ask them:

> ***Do you think spinning your wheel 10 times generates enough data to accurately reflect the statistics on your wheel? Why or why not?***

Allow your students to share their responses to this question. You will find that most agree that 10 spins isn't nearly enough. This realization presents you with an opportunity to discuss with your students how data can be skewed if too little of it is collected. You might ask how many times they would need to spin in order to get a more accurate reflection. Have them explain their reasoning for the number of spins they think they would need.

Tell your students that for the first part of this activity, you would like them to spin their wheel and tally the results for 100 spins. Before spinning however, they should talk with their partner and predict what they think their results will look like after spinning the player wheel 100 times. Suggest to your students that they use the wheel itself, the **Player Analysis Charts**, and the player's baseball card to help them with their predictions.

Once the students have made their predictions, have them share in small groups, telling why they made the predictions they did. After making their predictions, tell your students to go ahead and spin their wheel 100 times, recording each spin by using a tally mark. When they have completed their 100 spins, they can total the tallies for each statistic and record the results.

Have your students compare their results with their predictions and ask them to discuss the following questions:

> ***Are you surprised at your results? Did you come close in any of the statistical categories? Did you hit any exactly? Do you think you would get similar results if you spun the same player wheel another 100 times? Why or why not?***

Comparing Results — A Visual Comparison

When your students have finished discussing how their results compared to their predictions, you will want to have them begin to see how to make predictions based on an understanding of probability. Encourage them to compare the results of the 100 spins with their **Player Analysis Charts**. Do they see any similarities? You will probably get a mixed response to this. Some will notice that the results of their 100-spin experiment are related to the numbers found in the decimal equivalent section of the charts. (For example, 21 singles and .2408, 4 doubles and .0389, 0 triples and .0015 . . .). For others, however, the numbers will not appear close enough for them to see any relationship. Before you proceed to looking at probability, you may first want to do the following investigation with your students to help all of them see that some sort of relationship exists. This brief excursion provides a visual, geometric comparison between the results of 100 spins and the percentage of area each statistical category covers on the player wheel.

Pass out a sheet of 1-cm. graph paper to each pair of students. Tell them that you would like them to create a bar graph that represents the results of their 100 spins. Provide them with some very important guidelines before they begin constructing their graphs:

- The statistical categories labeled along the x axis of the graph should be in the order these categories appear on their player wheels (either clockwise or counter-clockwise).
- Each bar should be shaded in with a different colored pencil or marker.
- The scale along the y axis should progress by twos. This will most likely allow for all of the data to be recorded on one sheet of paper.

Once students have completed their graphs, explain how they will use these to compare the results with the player wheels they used. Instruct them to write the statistical category on each bar and then cut out each one to make a series of paper strips. Have them attach a white paper tab under one end of each strip, then glue the bars together (in order) so only the colored strips of paper can be seen.

When they are finished, your students should have one long strip of paper (50 total squares) that is made up of several different colors and has a small white tab at either the top or the bottom. Tell students to form a circle with this strip, gluing it together, so that the colored side is on the inside of the circle. Have them then lay this circle of paper over their player wheel so that the categories on the new circle graph align with the ones on the player wheels.

Have your students compare the results of their new graph with the player wheels. Some students will now be able to see that the results of their 100 spins matches very closely (in some categories) with the space on the player wheel. Others may find that the match is closer than it was with 10 spins, yet still does not accurately reflect the player wheel itself. To these students you might ask:

Would the circle graph get closer to matching your player wheel if you tallied more spins? Why or why not? How could you find out?

These questions will lead your students into the next part of this activity.

Determining Theoretical Probability

When your students made their predictions, some may have used the available statistics to make some educated guesses, perhaps simply seeing that there should be about twice as many strikeouts as walks, for example. Others may have seen the mathematical connection between the decimal equivalents in their **Player Analysis Charts** and the probable outcomes in spinning their player wheels 100 times. At this point, you want to help all your students see these mathematical connections.

Tell them that they are going to take a closer look at theoretical probability — or what the results of *x* number of spins should be if figured mathematically. Explain that the theoretical probability of spinning any statistical category on a player wheel can be determined by referring to the statistics from the **Player Analysis Charts** that the wheels were based on. The theoretical probability of an event is usually determined by the following equation:

$$\textbf{Probability of event} = \frac{\textbf{Number of ways the event can occur}}{\textbf{Total number of outcomes}}$$

For example, the probability of rolling a 3 with a six-sided die is $\frac{1}{6}$ because there is one way of rolling a 3 and six possible outcomes. When using the player wheels, determining the theoretical probability of spinning any one statistical category involves determining how much area that category covers on the spinner in relation to the total area covered by the spinner. One way to do this is to divide the number of degrees the category encompasses by 360 (the number of degrees on the spinner).

However, because the degrees on the player wheels were based on the decimal equivalents and ratios from the **Player Analysis Charts**, these numbers can be used as well. (These numbers will not yield results that are as accurate since the numbers were rounded when they were converted from fractions to decimals to degrees.) For the purposes of this experiment, however, your students may see that a shortcut in determining the theoretical probability of the statistical categories in 100 spins is to use the decimal equivalent section on their **Player Analysis Charts**.

To help your students see this, you may want to use the transparency of the **Player Analysis Chart** for Robin Ventura (from Activity 3) as a visual example:

Name	Cum. AB	H	1B	2B	3B	HR	BB	SO	Other Outs	FO	GO
Robin Ventura	686	172	123	25	1	23	80	67	367	183	184
RATIO			123/686	25/686	1/686	23/686	80/686	67/686		183/686	184/686
DECIMAL EQUIVALENT			.1793	.0364	.0014	.0335	.1166	.0976		.2667	.2682
DEGREES			65°	13°	0°	12°	42°	35°		96°	97°

Teacher Notes

I have sometimes let my students know that following their experiment, they may have the option of creating a new wheel for their one player based on the results from their experiment. This they will only want to do, of course, if the results yield better percentages than their original wheel.

Point out to your students that the decimal equivalent can be expressed as a percentage simply by multiplying it by 100. Then by rounding to the nearest hundredth, you can make the following predictions for Robin Ventura, which would represent the theoretical probability for each of the statistical categories.

My prediction for:

Robin Ventura

1B	2B	3B	HR	BB	SO	FO	GO
18	3	0	3	12	10	27	27

Predicting Results of 360 Spins

Pass out a copy of the **Theoretical vs. Experimental Probability** recording sheet to each student. Tell them that they will be completing the three sections one at a time, after some brief instruction given by you. Let them know that they will be using the data they produce on this worksheet to help them make predictions about what the results of their team's statistics will look like at the end of the Fantasy Baseball season.

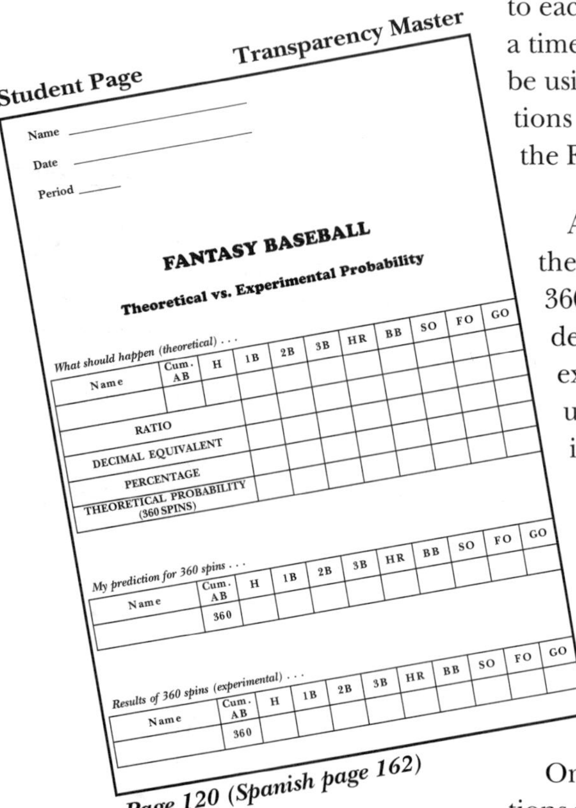
Student Page

Transparency Master

Name

Date

Period

FANTASY BASEBALL

Theoretical vs. Experimental Probability

What should happen (theoretical) . . .

Name	Cum. AB	H	1B	2B	3B	HR	BB	SO	FO	GO
RATIO										
DECIMAL EQUIVALENT										
PERCENTAGE										
THEORETICAL PROBABILITY (360 SPINS)										

My prediction for 360 spins . . .

Name	Cum. AB	H	1B	2B	3B	HR	BB	SO	FO	GO
	360									

Results of 360 spins (experimental) . . .

Name	Cum. AB	H	1B	2B	3B	HR	BB	SO	FO	GO
	360									

Page 120 (Spanish page 162)

Ask your students to look at the recording sheet and think of a reason why they might want to run an experiment with their wheel, spinning it exactly 360 times. Many will see that the number 360 is identical to the number of degrees in a circle. Let students know that they will use the results from their experiment to compare with their player's original **Player Analysis Chart**. By using 360 spins, they will easily be able to compare the theoretical probability with the experimental probability.

Point out to your students that they should fill in the theoretical probability section of their recording sheet with the mathematical determinations of what should happen if they spin their wheel 360 times. The actual results of 360 spins can be right on, close or way off. This would be a good time to show your students the results of your 360 spins and how they compare with the theoretical probability and your predictions.

Once you have had this discussion, have your students make their predictions for 360 spins. Remind them that their Cum. AB should be 360 and that the total of 1B, 2B, 3B, HR, BB, SO, FO and GO should equal 360. Your students may realize that the number of degrees for each statistical category of their player wheel can be divided by 360 to get the theoretical probability.

360 Spins — Looking At Experimental Probability

Once your students have finished making their predictions, it is time to for them to continue on with their experiment. Remind them that they have already spun their wheels 100 times and that these results will be added with the results of 260 more spins. You might suggest that they do their spins in two groups of 100 and one final group of 60. For fun, your students might want to predict what they think will happen prior to each group of spins. They can use the completed **Player Analysis Charts** and the results of each set of spins to help them alter their predictions for each new group of spins.

Provide the time (and possibly an incentive) for your students to complete the remaining three groups of spins to complete this part of the experiment. Once they have recorded each group of spins, have them total their results and enter the data on their recording sheets. Have them complete the chart labeled Results of 360 Spins and then compare these results to the theoretical probability they calculated and to their predictions.

Point out to your students that by running their experiment, they are able to determine a different type of probability, experimental probability. Provide them with the following definition: when a probability is determined from experience or by observing the results of experiments, it is called experimental probability. To clarify this, ask your students to compare the number of HR's their player theoretically should have received after spinning the player wheel 360 times to the number they actually got. If these numbers differ (which they most likely do), your students might determine the probability of spinning a HR either higher or lower, based on their results.

Have them compare the other categories to see how they match up. Allow them to share and compare with the other students seated in their small groups. As a reward for their efforts, give your students the option of using the results from their experiment to make a new wheel for their particular player. If they choose to construct a new wheel based on their results, the old wheel should be set aside and not used at all during the regular season.

Predicting End of Season Statistics

Remind your students that soon they will be starting the Fantasy Baseball regular season. Explain that during this season, they will be playing a minimum of 20 games against other teams in the classroom. Through the course of playing these games, they will be collecting and organizing each player's statistics to eventually compare them with their original **Player Analysis Charts**.

Teacher Notes

I was concerned that my students might get bored with spinning their wheels 260 more times. To spice things up, I ran some contests to help them generate this data. Working as a team, they tried to spin and tally as much data as they could in 3 minutes. I gave extra packages of baseball cards to the three teams that generated the highest number of spins in the three minutes. I repeated this process for 2 minutes and twice for 1 minute. Before I knew it, we had most of the 260 spins that we needed. Besides that, my students were excited to "win" additional packages of cards.

Teacher Notes

I decided to have my students in one class run this experiment with 200 spins rather than the 360 that was suggested. I chose 200 because that is the number of at bats that is required of an eligible player. For another class I had them spin the wheel the number of cumulative at bats the player had for the selected season. From these results, my students had to solve proportion problems to relate their experiment to 360 spins. I found this variation useful in reinforcing the interrelatedness of numbers and the number sense that this unit is built around.

Teacher Notes

I like to give my students a bit longer to think about what they've learned with regards to probability. Because of what they've experienced, the conversation around the classroom sounds quite a bit different as they make their predictions for the upcoming season. It's encouraging to see them referring to their *Player Analysis Charts* and doing mini-experiments with their player wheels prior to recording their predictions.

Tell your students that you would like them to predict what their players' statistics will look like after 20 games. Be sure to point out that they will not be graded for how close they get as their is no absolute way to determine what will happen.

At the end of 20 games, your students will be comparing their players' actual statistics to their predictions and **Player Analysis Charts** to see if their is any apparent relationship between the three.

Have your students use a **Team Stat Sheet** to record their predictions. In order to keep some consistency, ask your students to use the number 80 as the Cum. AB for their predictions. (This number will be fairly close — it represents four Cum. AB's for each player for the 20 games). Ask them to complete every section of the chart. In order to determine AVG., OB% and SLG. %, they may need to refer to resource materials they received or notes they took earlier in the unit. Once they have completed their predictions, they can be placed in their team envelopes or their Fantasy Baseball folder.

Transparency Master

Transparency Master

Activity 7 Manager's Log

In your own words, explain what you have done in class these past few days and what you have learned. Be sure to include as much as possible regarding what you've learned about probability.

Activity 8 Manager's Log

Write a short newspaper article that provides an update on what has happened with your baseball team. What is your record? How are individual players doing? Have you, as co-manager, made any recent decisions that have helped the team? What is the outlook for the next five games?

Unit Wrap Manager's Log

Write a paragraph or two on each of your three players, comparing the statistics on their baseball cards with the statistics you gathered during the regular season. Use your completed charts as tools to provide an accurate comparison of these statistics.

Page 121 (Spanish page 163)

Activity Wrap — Manager's Log

Ask your students to take out their journals and prepare to write to today's prompt. Tell them that they may want to keep out the materials they have used during the past two to three days to use as resources while working on this entry. Write the following on the overhead or chalkboard:

In your own words, explain what you have done in class these past few days and what you have learned. Be sure to include as much as possible regarding what you've learned about probability.

Provide your students with 10–15 minutes of "quiet time" to complete this entry in their log. If time allows, have them share their writing in small groups and possibly call on a few interested students to share with the class.

** At this point, you will want to have your students vote on the Regular Season Schedule they would like to use for their class. Allow your students to cast their vote from the selection of schedules (prepared by students) that you have available. Whichever schedule is selected should be used for Opening Day and throughout the entire regular season.

Looking Ahead

Let your students know that they will be participating in Opening Day ceremonies to kick off the regular season. Explain that they will be using the schedule that was voted on to play Fantasy Baseball games and gather individual player and team statistics. Along with playing regular season games, let your students know that each team (set of co-managers) will be responsible for maintaining a chart that keeps track of League Leaders in a variety of statistical categories.

ACTIVITY 8
REGULAR SEASON/COMPILING STATISTICS

◆ ◆ ◆

Summary

Opening Day kicks off the beginning of the Fantasy Baseball regular season. Students play a 20-game season where they have the opportunity to play every team in class at least once. The students also investigate ways to bring stolen bases into the game as well as other outcomes (bunts, sacrifices, double plays, etc.) They total player statistics after each game and complete a **Team Stat Sheet** after every five games. The **Team Stat Sheets** after 10, 15 and 20 games can be completed using a computer spreadsheet. Along with team statistics, students take responsibility for keeping track of League Leaders in an assortment of categories (e.g., hits, RBI's, HR's, etc.)

Math Content

- collecting, organizing, displaying and analyzing data
- operating with fractions/decimals/percents
- applying algebraic formulas (computer spreadsheet)
- designing structures for probabilistic events
- linear and exponential growth **(Challenge Problem #3)**

Classroom Time

12–15 days (These days do not need to be consecutive — this part of the unit can be done over a longer period of time.)

Materials

Student Pages:

Team Standings/Avg. Leaders (Examples) (1 per student)

Challenge Problem #3 (1 per student)

Transparencies:

Activity 8 Discussion Questions (After 5 Games — Investigating Stolen Bases)

Player Wheels (set for each team)

Scoresheets (blank)

Regular Season Schedule (from Activity 8)

Team Stat Sheets (4 per team)

Activity 8 Manager's Log transparency

Activity 8 Performance Assessment transparency

Calculators

Computers (optional - strongly recommended)

Manager's Log

Pre-Activity Preparation

There are many different ways that you can prepare for Opening Day of the Fantasy Baseball season. Each classroom will differ depending on how involved you want it to be. Some suggestions follow that you might choose to build upon. Give this some thought and solicit student input into designing Opening Day ceremonies for your particular classroom. Be sure to allow yourself 2–3 days of lead time to prepare for all of the necessary "hype."

Opening Day

This is the day that your students have been waiting for — Opening Day of the Fantasy Baseball regular season. There is no doubt that they will be ready to jump in and begin the season, all with high hopes of winning the league pennant, then the World Series.

Make sure that you have the **Regular Season Schedule** that the class voted to use posted in a highly visible place in the classroom. Your students will want to know who their first two games will be played against so they can direct some friendly taunting towards their opponents.

How you operate Opening Day in your classroom is entirely up to you. You may want to keep it simple or make it a major event. Below are some possible ideas that you can implement and/or modify to make your Opening Day one that the students will remember.

Teacher Notes

Opening Day is always a big deal to me and consequently, to my students. I get all decked out in my baseball garb and have a great time leading them through the ceremonies. Back in the classroom, I become a vendor slinging peanuts and Cracker Jacks around the room for $.25. The money collected goes into a fund to buy prizes for the League Champions and World Series Champions at the end of the season.

- Invite a local ballplayer as a guest speaker.
- Hold your ceremony outside at a baseball field.
- Have each team create a banner or pennant for Opening Day.
- Encourage students to wear baseball clothes advertising the team they manage.
- Sing the national anthem.
- Invite the principal or a local celebrity to throw out the first pitch.
- Sell peanuts and Cracker Jacks (cheap). Use the money collected for end-of-season prizes (pennants, hats, etc.)
- Have a cookout with hot dogs and soda.
- Sing *Take Me Out To The Ballgame* (7th inning stretch)
- Do the wave!
- Invite the media — get coverage of this historic event.

The list above is not all inclusive and you may have other ideas that will work better for your school situation. However you choose to handle the Opening Day ceremonies, the goal should be to provide your students with a positive experience that they'll never forget.

Once you have held your Opening Day ceremonies, you will want to have the students play their Opening Day game or games. You may choose to have them play only one game in order to facilitate the activities prior to playing the game. Let them know that on most days, however, they will be expected to complete two games against two different teams.

Regular Season (20 games)

A reasonable expectation for your students is to have them play 2 games during a 45–55 minute class period. What works well is to establish a 20–25 minute time limit for each game. Students are then required to play at least 5 innings for the game to be official. Structuring the time in class helps to keep teams moving along at a reasonable clip in an organized manner. Playing two games per period, your students won't always be able to total their player stats at the end of the game. This is something that can be completed for homework as long as it is done prior to playing any games the following day. It is important that your students maintain an up-to-date record of the game totals to avoid having to play catch-up when it's time to complete a **Team Stat Sheet**.

Make sure that your students follow the **Regular Season Schedule** as closely as possible. Occasionally you will need to make modifications due to absences or unanticipated interruptions that come up. Be sure to let your students know that they are able to make decisions that they feel would benefit their teams. Prior to any game, they can change their lineup, if they feel it would be in the best interest of the team. Encourage your managers to confer on strategies that they feel would help their teams accumulate victories.

Teacher Notes

It is remarkable how adept students become at keeping score and talking strategy after only a few games. At this point, it's fun to go back and read the writing and pre-assessment the students completed at the beginning of the unit. Without exception, you will be able to note a considerable amount of growth in your students' knowledge, conceptual understandings and attitude. It is also a good time to provide additional strokes to those students that have overcome their initial reluctance to accept this unit as anything of value to them. You will probably recognize them as the ones you can't tear away from the games long enough to speak to them!

Team Stat Sheets

At the conclusion of 5 games, have your students complete a **Team Stat Sheet** for their respective teams. This sheet should include each player's totals for the 5 games. You may want to have each co-manager complete a sheet so that one can be kept by the team and one can be turned in to you. This allows you to keep track of each team's progress and also provides a resource for students when they begin charting League Leaders in each statistical category.

Explain to your students that they will be expected to update their totals after 10, 15 and 20 games. If you have access to a computer spreadsheet program, you may want to let them know that after they complete this first **Team Stat Sheet**, they will not be responsible for calculating each player's AVG., OB%, and SLG%. They will be learning how to use a computer spreadsheet that gives them access to these statistics in a fraction of the time it would take to calculate them. They will be using the spreadsheet for this purpose after 10, 15 and 20 games.

Team Standings/League Leaders

Each team in your classroom should be given the responsibility to maintain a League Chart that is updated after every 5 games. You may want to exempt the team that created the **Regular Season Schedule** that the class is using. Each of these charts will provide your students with statistical information of interest to them. One team will need to be responsible for keeping the **Team Standings** and updating their chart after every set of games. Make it clear that the students will need to report their scores after each game to the managers in charge of the standings.

Student Page

FANTASY BASEBALL

Team Standings/Avg. Leaders

(Examples)

FANTASY BASEBALL

TEAM STANDINGS

American League				National League			
TEAM	W	L	PCT.	TEAM	W	L	PCT.
Tigers	5	0	1.000	Cardinals	4	1	.800
Orioles	4	1	.800	Padres	4	1	.800
Twins	4	1	.800	Giants	3	2	.600
Royals	3	2	.600	Expos	2	3	.400
Yankees	3	2	.600	Mets	1	4	.200
Indians	2	3	.400	Cubs	0	5	.000
Rangers	0	5	.000	Dodgers	0	5	.000

FANTASY BASEBALL

BATTING AVERAGE LEADERS

NAME	TEAM	AVERAGE
Lou Whitaker	Tigers	.583
Will Clark	Mets	.514
Wade Boggs	Indians	.474
Frank Thomas	Twins	.459
Andre Dawson	Giants	.406
Barry Bonds	Cardinals	.388
Ken Griffey Jr.	Cardinals	.372
Gary Sheffield	Orioles	.351
Tony Gwynn	Rangers	.349
Paul Molitor	Padres	.333

Page 122 (Spanish page 164)

The following 13 statistical categories can also be charted under the heading **League Leaders**: At Bats, Runs, Hits, Doubles, Triples, Home Runs, Bases on Balls, Strikeouts, Batting Average, On-Base Percentage, Slugging Average, Stolen Bases and Runs Batted In. You may want to pass out copies of the **Team Standings/Avg. Leaders (Examples)** charts to your students to show them one way they might organize this information.

By creating a Fantasy Baseball bulletin board in your classroom, your students will be able to display their charts for the whole class to see. Make sure to have students update these charts after every five (5) games in order to keep the most current information available. Keep a folder with each team's updated **Team Stat Sheet** (the one turned in to you) available for your students to use as a resource when updating their charts.

After 5 Games — Investigating Stolen Bases

After playing 5 regular season games and completing their first **Team Stat Sheet**, your students are most likely getting very comfortable with the Fantasy Baseball games. Now is the time to throw a "curve" and get them involved in making modifications that will enhance the game. Stolen bases, is just one of many aspects of the game of baseball that can be explored to continue drawing out the rich mathematics in baseball. You may want to consider a break after 10 games to investigate bunts and after 15 games to investigate double plays and have your students devise a way to bring these into their Fantasy Baseball games.

Point out to your students that on the backs of their baseball cards they will find a statistic that you have probably ignored up to this point, SB or stolen bases. Many of your students will know what stolen bases are and should be given the chance to explain to others in the class that don't know. Tell your students that you figure they have had enough experiences with spinners and dice that you would like them to explore different ways for bringing stolen bases into the Fantasy Baseball games. At this point, you want them to devise a method that uses their mathematical understanding of probability and statistics.

Insist that your students work together in groups of four to develop a method for including stolen bases that they feel would be fair. Although they may all have great ideas, they must arrive at consensus for their group method. Let them know that they will be expected to present their final products to the class as well as the reasoning that went behind them. At the conclusion of this sharing, each team will have the option to adopt a "home ballpark" method that will be used during games when they are the home team.

Before turning your students loose on this investigation, you may want to present them with a few questions that will help guide their group discussions. Here are some things they might want to consider:

- ***Are all base runners equally adept at stealing bases?***
- ***Should everyone have the same chances of success?***
- ***Are some bases easier to steal than others?***
- ***Can more than one runner steal a base at a time?***
- ***Can a runner steal more than one base at a time?***
- ***Are there any bases that can't be stolen?***
- ***Are there any situations where a runner cannot steal a base?***
- ***How can we use the information on the baseball cards to help us create our method?***

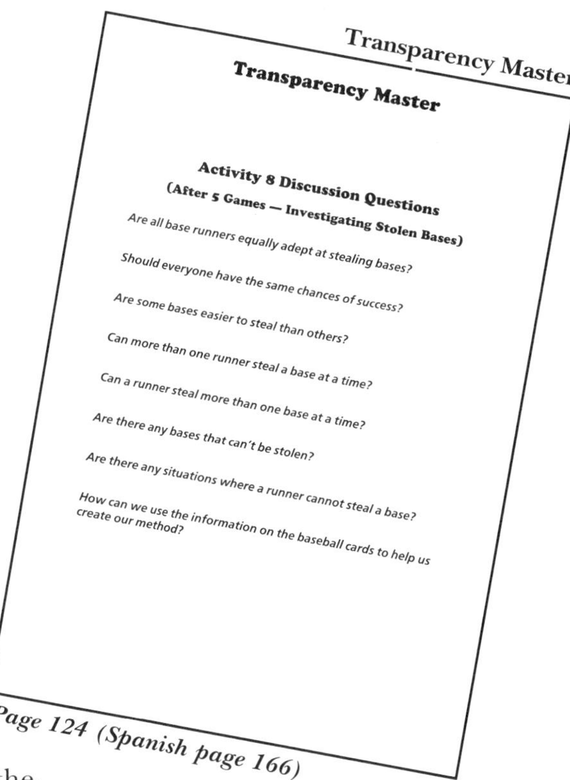
Transparency Master

Transparency Master

Activity 8 Discussion Questions
(After 5 Games — Investigating Stolen Bases)

Are all base runners equally adept at stealing bases?

Should everyone have the same chances of success?

Are some bases easier to steal than others?

Can more than one runner steal a base at a time?

Can a runner steal more than one base at a time?

Are there any bases that can't be stolen?

Are there any situations where a runner cannot steal a base?

How can we use the information on the baseball cards to help us create our method?

Page 124 (Spanish page 166)

Once you have presented and possibly had some discussion about some of these questions, have the groups start on their investigations. Provide a time structure that you are comfortable with them to work within and then allow for them to present their consensus-based methods to the class. Make clear to your students that you want them to explain their mathematical reasoning behind their methods. In the same way that you had our students discuss the merits of the Pitcher Batting Guide, encourage your students to critique their strategies for incorporating stolen bases. The main questions they should be asking are: Does it make sense mathematically? Does it keep the game fair and challenging (or does it lead to managers always trying to steal a base or never trying to steal a base)? At the conclusion of the presentations, each team needs to select a method for implementing stolen bases that will become part of their "home ballpark" rules.

Teacher Notes

We ended up spending three days on this investigation. Two days were spent working in the groups and one day was set aside for presentations and discussion. I was astounded at how intricate some of their methods were. This was a great way to begin to assess what the students had learned throughout the unit. It also gave them that additional buy-in to the games as they took on the roles of authors and developers.

Team Stats — Computer Spreadsheet (if available)

Once your students have completed their tenth game of the regular season, they should complete a revised **Team Stat Sheet**. Before doing this, explain to them that you would like them to complete every column except for Avg., OB% and SLG%. Tell them that they are going to learn to use a computer spreadsheet that will not only help to organize and display their data, but will also perform the calculations for these statistics very quickly.

You will need to experiment with whatever spreadsheet program you have at your disposal prior to presenting this activity to your students. Your students will need to input the data for all of the statistics on the **Team Stat Sheet** except for Avg., OB % and SLG%. The formulas needed to calculate these statistics are:

$$\text{Avg.} = \frac{H}{AB}$$

$$\text{OB\%} = \frac{(H + BB)}{(AB + BB)}$$

$$\text{SLG.\%} = \frac{(H) - (2B + 3B + HR) + 2(2B) + 3(3B) + 4(HR)}{AB}$$

Teacher Notes

I like to take the opportunity to talk with my students about how announcers and statisticians use the spreadsheet as a tool in their jobs. I ask students to watch or listen to a baseball game, looking for times when an announcer says, "If Barry gets two more hits in his next two at-bats, his average will be up over .350" or something like this. I explain that by having access to a spreadsheet, these announcers can quickly find out this type of information and pass it along to their listeners.

You will want to program the spreadsheet so that each of these statistics is carried out to only three (3) decimal places. Once your students have input their data after 10 games into the computer, they can print out a copy of their completed spreadsheet. By saving their file, they can return to this spreadsheet after 15 games and make changes in the data they've collected during the most recent 5 games. They will be amazed at how quickly the computer will change the calculations for AVG., OB% and SLG% based on the new data that is input. Students can again print a copy of their spreadsheet and repeat this process a final time after completing their twentieth game.

Challenge Problem #3: Salary Hike — 2000

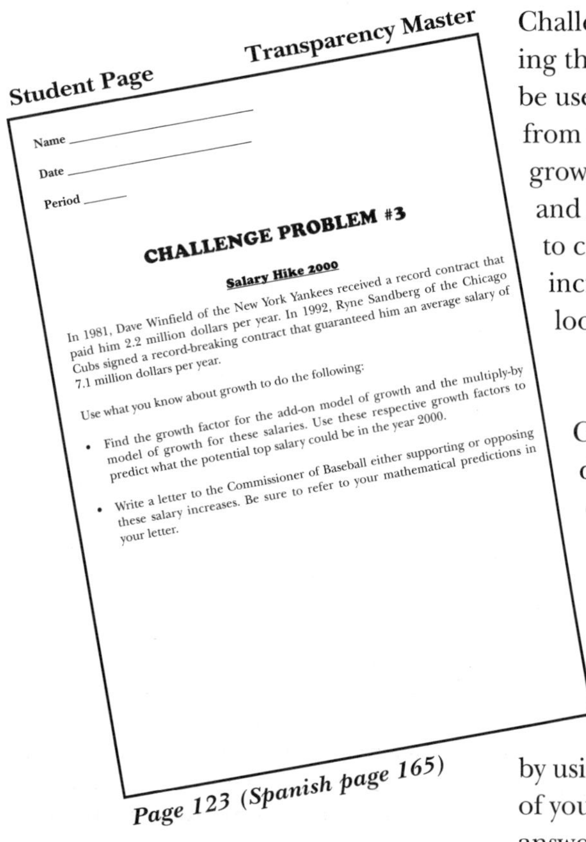
Student Page — Transparency Master

Name ______

Date ______

Period ______

CHALLENGE PROBLEM #3

Salary Hike 2000

In 1981, Dave Winfield of the New York Yankees received a record contract that paid him 2.2 million dollars per year. In 1992, Ryne Sandberg of the Chicago Cubs signed a record-breaking contract that guaranteed him an average salary of 7.1 million dollars per year.

Use what you know about growth to do the following:

- Find the growth factor for the add-on model of growth and the multiply-by model of growth for these salaries. Use these respective growth factors to predict what the potential top salary could be in the year 2000.
- Write a letter to the Commissioner of Baseball either supporting or opposing these salary increases. Be sure to refer to your mathematical predictions in your letter.

Page 123 (Spanish page 165)

Challenge Problem #3 is included with this activity as another break from playing the Fantasy Baseball games and looking at statistics. Like the first two, it can be used as a Problem of the Week that is processed as a group roughly five days from when it is passed out. It involves working with linear and exponential growth, understanding the density of rational numbers, working with functions and roots, and looking at relationships between graphs. It also allows students to creatively craft a letter either supporting or opposing potential salary increases. Before handing out Challenge Problem #3, you may want to review looking at growth patterns for determining linear and exponential growth.

The following questions are provided to assist you with processing this Challenge Problem with your students. You may choose to present your students with some of these questions as they are grappling with the problem or strictly use them to process the problem upon completion. These questions are not all inclusive - while working through the problem you may discover others that would be of benefit to your students. Write them down and use them. Again, try to pull as much mathematics from the problem as you possibly can.

Please encourage your students to solve the pieces of this problem by using methods/strategies that are comfortable and make sense to them. All of your students will benefit from seeing the variety of approaches used to answer these questions.

What is the difference (in dollars) between Dave Winfield's contract and Ryne Sandberg's?

How many years passed between the signing of their contracts? If record contracts increased the same amount each year between 1981 and 1992, how much did they increase each year? Using this linear approach, what would the salary be in 1983? 1987? 1990?

If this linear growth continued, what would the top salary be in 1995? 1998? 2000? If you were to graph the salaries for the years 1981–2000, what would your graph look like?

If salaries were increased by a certain percentage each year as opposed to a set dollar amount, how would this affect the rate at which salaries grow? Explain your reasoning.

How many numbers are there between 1.1 and 1.2? Write down as many as you can in one minute. Explain why your examples fit between 1.1 and 1.2.

What growth factor would you multiply by to grow from 2.2 million in 1981 to 7.1 million in 1992? How did you arrive at this growth factor?

If this exponential growth continued, what would the top salary be in 1995? 1998? 2000? If you were to graph the salaries for the years 1981–2000, what would this graph look like?

What are the similarities and differences between the linear growth graph and the exponential growth graph? Explain why the differences occur.

Is this a good problem? Why or why not?

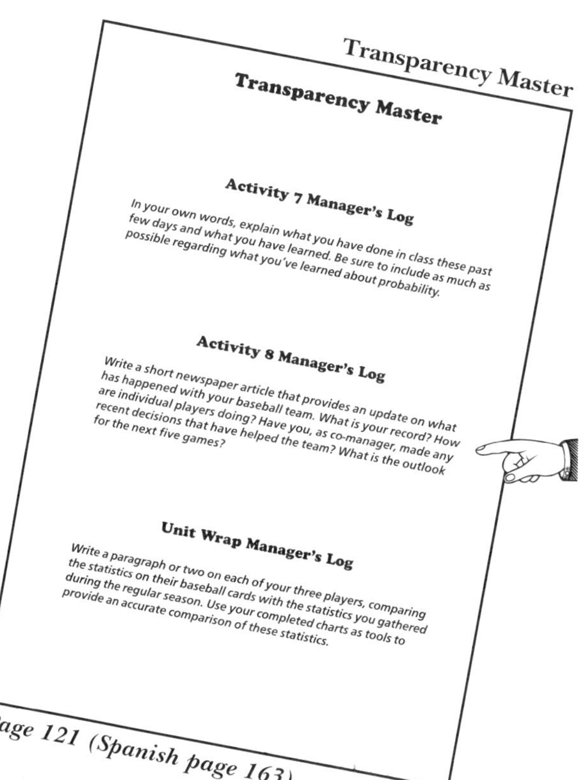
Transparency Master

Transparency Master

Activity 7 Manager's Log

In your own words, explain what you have done in class these past few days and what you have learned. Be sure to include as much as possible regarding what you've learned about probability.

Activity 8 Manager's Log

Write a short newspaper article that provides an update on what has happened with your baseball team. What is your record? How are individual players doing? Have you, as co-manager, made any recent decisions that have helped the team? What is the outlook for the next five games?

Unit Wrap Manager's Log

Write a paragraph or two on each of your three players, comparing the statistics on their baseball cards with the statistics you gathered during the regular season. Use your completed charts as tools to provide an accurate comparison of these statistics.

Page 121 (Spanish page 163)

Manager's Log

After your students have completed their **Team Stat Sheets** following each five game increment, have them respond to the following writing prompt in their Manager's Log:

> ***Write a short newspaper article that provides an update on what has happened with your baseball team. What is your record? How are individual players doing? Have you, as co-manager, made any recent decisions that has helped the team? What is the outlook for the next five games?***

Your students may need more than the usual 10 minutes to complete this log entry. You may want to consider putting together a Fantasy Baseball Newspaper after every 5 or 10 games that can be published and passed out to every manager to keep them abreast of what is happening with every team.

Teacher Notes

I figured that this would be a great opportunity to integrate mathematics and writing. The language arts teacher at my school worked with me on this and gave our students credit for creating a bi-weekly Fantasy Baseball newsletter. The students got a kick out of writing their articles and it was a great method of communication with parents.

Activity Wrap — Final Season Statistics

If you are electing to wrap up the Fantasy Baseball season after 20 regular season games, you will want your students to go to the spreadsheet one final time. By including their players' statistics for the final 5 games, they should be able to print out a final **Team Stat Sheet** that reflects the 20-game season. If you plan to include Fantasy Baseball in your curriculum throughout the school year, you will still want your students to include these statistics in their spreadsheet and print out a 20-game **Team Stat Sheet**. This will be used during the unit wrap and can also be included in students' **Open-Ended Assessment** to be done at the conclusion of the unit.

** Be sure to have your students write to the Manager's Log prompt upon completion of gathering their teams' end-of-season statistics.

Transparency Master

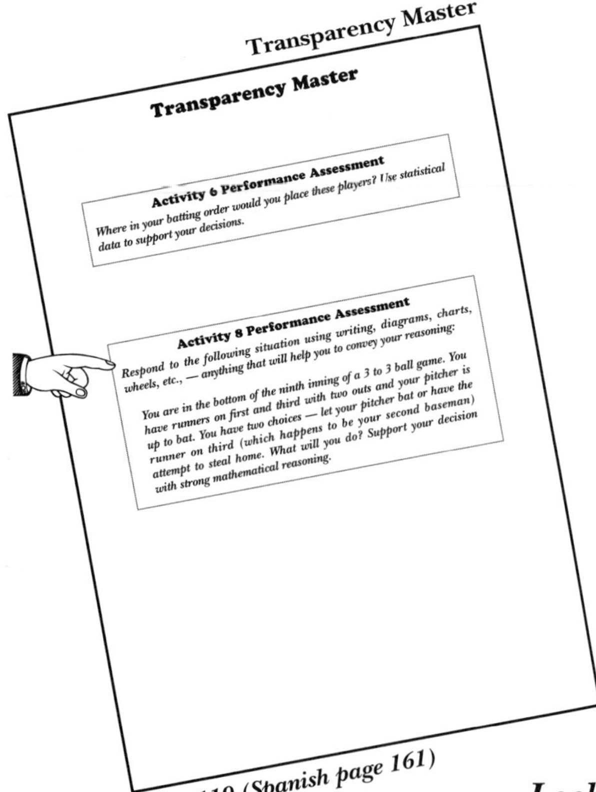

Transparency Master

Activity 6 Performance Assessment

Where in your batting order would you place these players? Use statistical data to support your decisions.

Activity 8 Performance Assessment

Respond to the following situation using writing, diagrams, charts, wheels, etc., — anything that will help you to convey your reasoning:

You are in the bottom of the ninth inning of a 3 to 3 ball game. You have runners on first and third with two outs and your pitcher is up to bat. You have two choices — let your pitcher bat or have the runner on third (which happens to be your second baseman) attempt to steal home. What will you do? Support your decision with strong mathematical reasoning.

Page 119 (Spanish page 161)

Performance Assessment

Have your students respond to the following situation using writing, diagrams, charts, wheels, etc., anything that will help them to convey their reasoning.

You are in the bottom of the ninth inning of a 3 to 3 ballgame. You have runners on first and third with two outs and your pitcher is up to bat. You have two choices — let your pitcher bat or have the runner on third (who happens to be your second baseman) attempt to steal home. What will you do? Support your decision with strong mathematical reasoning.

Looking Ahead

Let your students know that they will be comparing their players' final statistics with the **Player Analysis Charts** and predictions they made earlier in the unit. If you're completing this unit during the baseball season, mention that they might also be looking in the newspapers to see how their players are doing during the current year. Explain that this will start the process of bringing the unit to a close before they complete an **Individual Assessment** and work with their co-manager on a unit culminating **Open-Ended Assessment**.

Unit Wrap
Analysis/Comparison of Statistics

◆ ◆ ◆

Summary

Students do a final compilation of their players' statistics from the 20 game regular season. They update their spreadsheet and have a printout available to compare with their season predictions and original **Player Comparison Charts** and **Player Analysis Charts**. If students are doing this unit during the Major League Baseball regular season, they may research their players' statistics for the current year and compare them with their statistics from Fantasy Baseball.

Math Connections

- number and operations
- algebra
- probability
- statistical analysis
- logic and language

Classroom Time

2–3 days

Materials

Transparencies:
  Unit Wrap Discussion Questions (Activity Wrap — Manager's Log)
Team Stat Sheet (with regular season predictions)
Player Comparison Charts (completed & blank)
Player Analysis Charts (completed & blank)
Team Stat Sheet (final spreadsheet results)
Unit Wrap Manager's Log transparency
Calculators
Daily newspapers (optional)
Manager's Log

Pre-Wrap Preparation

Make sure that the students' team envelopes (with all completed work) are available for their review. Also, run off enough copies of the **Player Comparison Charts** and **Player Analysis Charts** so that each student can receive a copy of each. If you are doing this unit during the Major League Baseball regular season and have access to newspapers, you may want to bring in copies of the Sunday paper. These often contain the statistics of all players for each of the Major League teams.

Reviewing Player Charts/Final Spreadsheet

Your students should have completed a minimum of 20 regular season games prior to starting this activity. Make sure that they have all of their previously completed work available for their review. Explain that you are going to give them some time to look back through their **Player Comparison Charts**, **Player Analysis Charts**, **Team Stat Sheet** (regular season predictions) and final **Team Stat Sheet** (spreadsheet) in preparation for doing a final comparison of three players of their choice. Allow your students about 20–25 minutes to review these materials with their co-managers. Stress to your students to try and reach some general conclusions about how their players fared during the regular season without getting too specific.

Comparing Statistics — 3 Players

Explain to your students that you would like them to do a thorough comparison of three of their players' statistics. The purpose of these comparisons is to see how closely each player's results are aligned with the theoretical probability that exists from the statistics on their baseball cards. You might mention that by having each co-manager compare three different players, the majority of Fantasy Baseball players will be reviewed. Let them know that if they would like, they can compare the remaining players on their teams if they have the time and/or desire to do so.

Pass out a blank copy of the **Player Comparison Chart** and the **Player Analysis Chart** to each student. Explain that they are to complete these charts for each of their three players based on their final statistics recorded on their spreadsheets. They should complete each section of these charts so that they will be able to accurately compare the data they started with along with the data they collected during the regular season. Allow students the time necessary to complete the charts for their players. Encourage them to confer with their co-manager if they run into any difficulties completing their charts.

Using the Newspaper (optional)

If you are doing this unit during baseball season, you may have the opportunity to make use of the newspaper while doing these comparisons. Major newspapers often contain player statistics for every Major League team in the Sunday newspaper. If you have access to this, you may want to have students look up their players in the paper and have their current statistics available when they do their written comparison. Be aware, students will need to search for some of their players as some will have been traded since the release of the baseball cards and will be playing for different teams. Having access to these statistics will add an additional dimension to their comparisons when writing in their Manager's Log.

Activity Wrap — Manager's Log

Have your students take out their Manager's Log. Explain to them that this entry will be more involved than most others and therefore will require more time. Assure them that they will be given enough time to complete this entry to their satisfaction. Stress to them that it is important that they take their time and do as complete a job as possible.

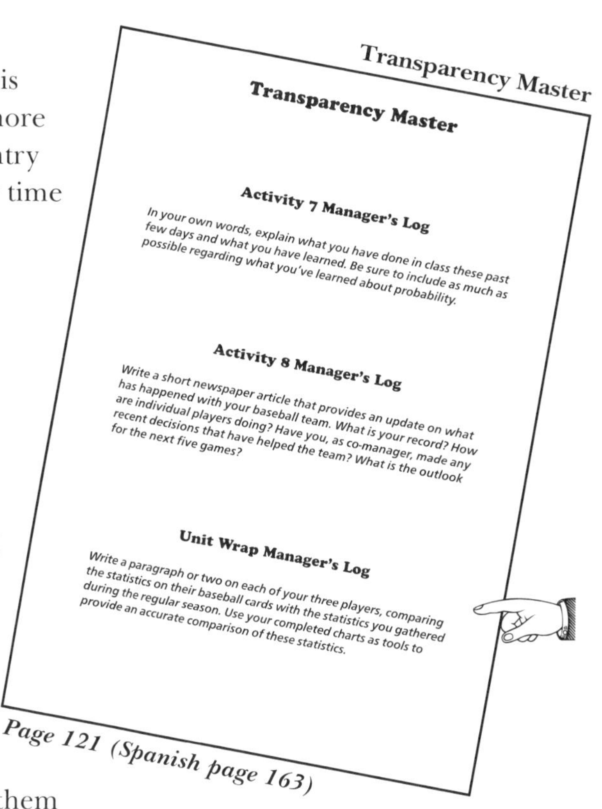
Transparency Master

Transparency Master

Activity 7 Manager's Log

In your own words, explain what you have done in class these past few days and what you have learned. Be sure to include as much as possible regarding what you've learned about probability.

Activity 8 Manager's Log

Write a short newspaper article that provides an update on what has happened with your baseball team. What is your record? How are individual players doing? Have you, as co-manager, made any recent decisions that have helped the team? What is the outlook for the next five games?

Unit Wrap Manager's Log

Write a paragraph or two on each of your three players, comparing the statistics on their baseball cards with the statistics you gathered during the regular season. Use your completed charts as tools to provide an accurate comparison of these statistics.

Page 121 (Spanish page 163)

Write the following on the chalkboard or overhead:

> ***Write a paragraph or two on each of your three players, comparing the statistics on their baseball cards with the statistics you gathered during the regular season. Use your completed charts as tools to provide an accurate comparison of these statistics.***

Provide your students with a quiet environment, conducive to completing this writing task. Allow anywhere from 20–30 minutes for the completion of this writing task. When all of your students have completed their entry, allow them to share the comparison for one of their players in their small groups.

If you have some additional time prior to the end of class, you may want to pose one or all of the following questions to your students. Allow them to engage in a whole class discussion on some or all of the following:

> ***If you were to begin a new Fantasy Baseball season, would you keep your current player wheels or make new ones based on their new statistics? Explain your choice.***
>
> ***Do you think your players would have better or worse statistics if they were to play 25 more games? Explain your reasoning.***
>
> ***After playing 20 regular season games of Fantasy Baseball, do you feel that the placement of statistical categories had any impact on the results? Why or why not?***
>
> ***Would you do anything differently regarding placement of statistics if you had to create new player wheels? If so, what would you do?***

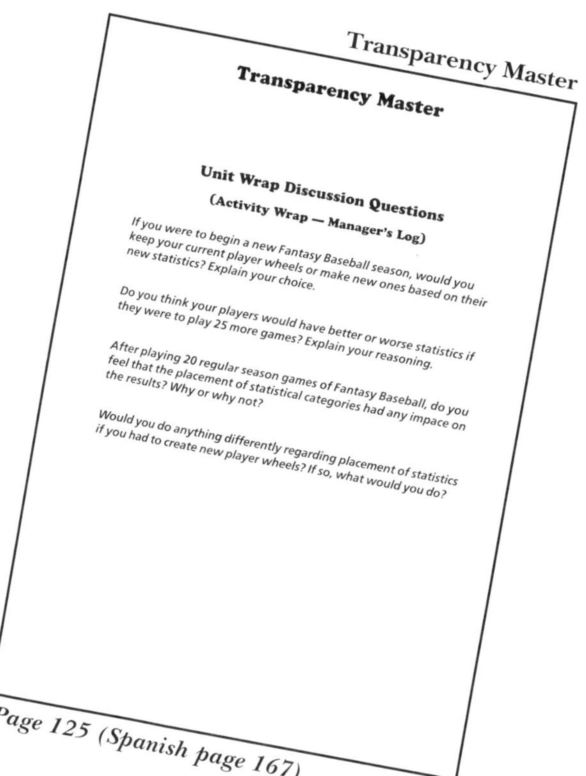
Transparency Master

Transparency Master

Unit Wrap Discussion Questions
(Activity Wrap — Manager's Log)

If you were to begin a new Fantasy Baseball season, would you keep your current player wheels or make new ones based on their new statistics? Explain your choice.

Do you think your players would have better or worse statistics if they were to play 25 more games? Explain your reasoning.

After playing 20 regular season games of Fantasy Baseball, do you feel that the placement of statistical categories had any impace on the results? Why or why not?

Would you do anything differently regarding placement of statistics if you had to create new player wheels? If so, what would you do?

Page 125 (Spanish page 167)

Looking Ahead

Let your students know that tomorrow they will be working on the first of two end-of-unit assessment pieces. Explain that they will be asked to individually investigate a situation similar to the unit pre-assessment: **New Kids In Town**. Let them know that they will have an entire class period to work on this individual assessment. Also, you may mention that they will have access to any materials they feel would be useful to help them complete this assessment.

Individual Assessment
"Free Agent Deal"

◆ ◆ ◆

Summary

Students complete a written assessment similar to the pre-assessment done at the beginning of the unit. They work individually and are provided with any tools they have used during the unit to help them with their response. This assessment is used to determine how well students have developed an understanding of analyzing statistics as well as compared with their pre-assessment to measure growth.

Mathematical Connections

Number & Operation
Algebra
Geometry
Measurement
Probability
Statistical Analysis
Logic & Language
Discrete Math

Classroom Time

1 day

Materials

Student Pages:
 Free Agent Deal (1 per student)
Player Comparison Charts (blank)
Player Analysis Charts (blank)
Player Wheels (blank)
Colored cardstock
Compasses
Protractors
Calculators
Paper and pencils
Scissors
Paper clips
Masking tape
Markers/crayons/colored pencils

Assessment Preparation

Make sure that you have plenty of the materials mentioned above available for each table of students. They will need to have easy access to these materials during the time allotted for completing this assessment. Also, have their team envelopes readily available for their review during the first 15 minutes of class.

Reviewing Team Folders

Let your students know that in approximately 15 minutes, you are going to ask them to complete an individual assessment, similar to the pre-assessment they took at the beginning of this unit. Assure them that you are confident that they will have more to offer in their responses this time around and that for this reason, they will be given approximately 45 minutes. In order to get their minds prepared for this assessment, explain that they will have 15 minutes to review the materials in their team envelopes. You might want to suggest that as they review the materials, that they quiz each other on different tasks they have completed during the unit. This is their opportunity to refresh their memories about what they've done to prepare for this assessment.

Student Page

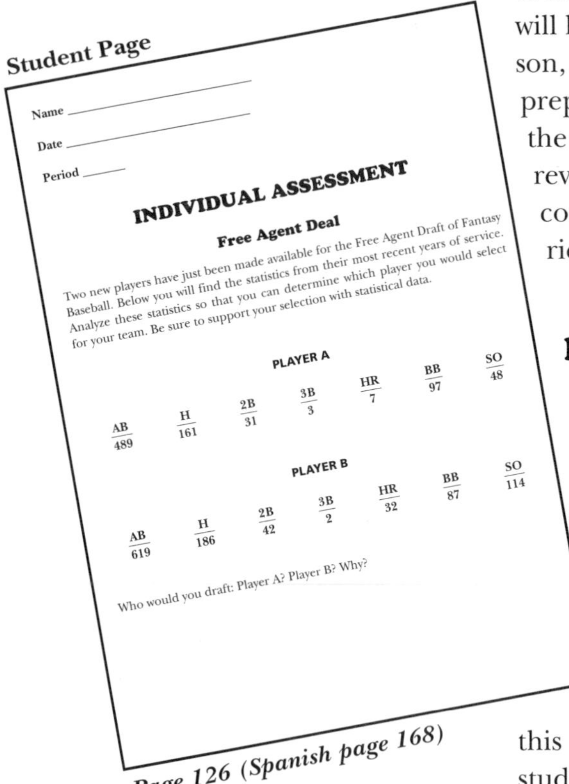

Name __________

Date __________

Period _____

INDIVIDUAL ASSESSMENT

Free Agent Deal

Two new players have just been made available for the Free Agent Draft of Fantasy Baseball. Below you will find the statistics from their most recent years of service. Analyze these statistics so that you can determine which player you would select for your team. Be sure to support your selection with statistical data.

PLAYER A

AB	H	2B	3B	HR	BB	SO
489	161	31	3	7	97	48

PLAYER B

AB	H	2B	3B	HR	BB	SO
619	186	42	2	32	87	114

Who would you draft: Player A? Player B? Why?

Page 126 (Spanish page 168)

Individual Assessment — "Free Agent Deal"

Pass out a copy of the assessment **"Free Agent Deal"** to each student. Also, make sure that they have plenty of materials available at their table for use on this assessment.

Read through this assessment with your students, clarifying any questions that they may have. Be sure to point out that they are to respond to the questions as completely as possible and that their responses are to be written on a separate sheet(s) of paper. Make it clear to your students that they may use any of the materials at their table to complete this assessment, as long as it is done individually, with no discussion. Let your students know that they'll have approximately 45 minutes to complete this task.

It is incredibly rewarding to watch the students go after this problem with their assorted strategies. What's exciting is that every student has developed understandings they lacked prior to the unit that help them attack this assessment. This is where all of the pieces of the puzzle come together for the students and you can see their increased levels of confidence and conceptual understanding.

If you have the availability of some extra time, allow the students to share their methods for approaching this problem with the entire class. This is an opportunity for students to show off what they know and tends to be an extremely positive experience for the presenters and their audience. Be sure to acknowledge the creativity and assortment of strategies that your students will use to write their responses to this assessment. After sharing, this student work should be collected for your review, then placed in your students' individual portfolios.

Teacher Notes

I found that 45 minutes wasn't long enough for some of my students to complete everything they wanted to do for this assessment. I decided to give whoever wanted an extra class period to complete the assessment. I did not want to limit them when they were so involved in the task. Those that didn't need or want the time got together with another student and played a game just for fun.

Looking Ahead

Let your students know that soon they will be starting a final assessment piece to the unit, this one with their co-managers. Explain that they will be able to apply all that they've learned from the unit in an **Open-Ended Project**.

Pair Assessment
Open-Ended Project

◆ ◆ ◆

Summary

Students work with their co-managers to complete an open-ended project outside of the classroom. This project enables students to apply everything they have learned from experiencing the unit. Two days of classroom time are set aside for small group presentations of the projects.

Mathematical Connections

Number & Operation
Algebra
Geometry
Measurement
Probability
Statistical Analysis
Logic & Language
Discrete Math

Classroom Time

2 days (for presentations only)

Materials

Student Pages:

Fantasy Baseball Project — An Open-Ended Assessment (1 per student)
Fantasy Baseball Project — Board Comments sheets (3 or more per student)

All materials used during the course of the unit should be made available to the students. This includes copies of any forms or charts that were used, as well as manipulative materials. Any additional materials needed by the students will either have to be negotiated with you or supplied by the students themselves.

Assessment Preparation

Be sure to have a copy of the **Fantasy Baseball Project — An Open-Ended Assessment** for each student. Also, any materials used during the unit should be made available for student use.

Student Page

FANTASY BASEBALL PROJECT

An Open-Ended Assessment

Situation:
You and your partner have just been hired as consultants for a major publishing firm. They have heard about a math unit called **Fantasy Baseball** and are seeking your help to learn more about the unit. If they consider the unit to be worthwhile, they intend to publish and market it under the company name. The publishing firm has two major concerns:

1. They want to be sure that the unit contains plenty of mathematics suitable for the students that participate in the unit.
2. They want to be sure that students are given the opportunity to communicate with others and use their creativity while participating in the unit.

Remember, the publisher knows very little about the unit — this is why you have been hired on by the firm.

Your Task
Create a display that explains what the **Fantasy Baseball** unit is all about. This display should include samples, illustrations, written descriptions, etc. — anything that will help the publisher get a clear picture of the unit. Be sure to give a great deal of consideration to the two concerns mentioned above. You may wish to gather additional information about your own **Fantasy Baseball** team to help with designing your display.

Be prepared to give a 3–5 minute presentation to the Board of Directors, providing them with the information they need to make a decision on whether or not to publish this unit. You will be evaluated by the Board on the clarity of your presentation, along with your visual and written display.

Page 127 (Spanish page 169)

Pair Assessment — Fantasy Baseball Project

Pass out a copy of the **Fantasy Baseball Project — An Open-Ended Assessment** to each student. Read through the instructions with your class, allowing students to ask any questions that they may have about the assessment. Let your students know that they will have five (5) school days to complete this project and that the majority of the work will need to be done outside of class. Inform them that they will be expected to give a 3-5 minute presentation to the class, presenting their final product. Explain that this is their final opportunity to put everything they have learned together to paint a clear, complete picture of the Fantasy Baseball unit.

* **Special Note:** You may want to allow your students class time to work on these projects if it is difficult for them to get together outside of school. Another option is to hold a couple of lunchtime and/or after school work sessions to allow students a structured time and place to get together with their partners.

Class Presentations

Structure your two days of presentation time so that each pair of students is allowed approximately 5 minutes to present their **Fantasy Baseball Project** to the rest of the class. These presentations should be done as if the students were presenting the unit to the Board of Directors of a large publishing firm. The students in the audience should be expected to be active listeners and have the opportunity to ask questions of the presenters at the conclusion of each presentation. Following these questions, have them complete a brief evaluation of the project and presentation they have just witnessed. You can use the **Fantasy Baseball Project — Board Comments** sheets for these evaluations, which can then be collected, reviewed by you, then passed out to the presenters to provide them with peer feedback on their efforts.

Student Page

Manager(s): ______

FANTASY BASEBALL PROJECT
Board Comments

Presentation: ______

Display: ______

Manager(s): ______

FANTASY BASEBALL PROJECT
Board Comments

Presentation: ______

Display: ______

Page 128 (Spanish page 170)

Displaying Student Projects

Put the students' Fantasy Baseball projects on display in the classroom or in the school library. Invite their parents to school to view the assortment of student work. You can use these projects as another means to assess your students' understandings of the mathematical content presented during the unit. They can also be used to measure the students' growth from their first experiences in the unit to the present. Photographs of the students' displays and photocopies of their written work can then be placed in their individual math portfolios.

Extending the Season
A Year-Long Option

◆ ◆ ◆

Depending on time of year you are working on this unit, you may choose to extend the Fantasy Baseball season. If you are starting the year with the unit, it is possible (and exciting to students), if the unit is carried on throughout the year. A new schedule can be created so that students have the opportunity to play at least one game per week. As it was done during the unit, students can return to the computer to update their spreadsheets after every five games. Team Standings and League Leader charts can also be maintained throughout the year.

Towards the end of the school year, dates and times can be set aside for the two teams with the best won-loss record in each league (regardless of what division they're in), to play in a League Championship Series. The winner of this series is the first team to win 4 out of 7 possible games. The two league winners (one American, one National) can then square off in the World Series. Again, the winner of the World Series is the first team to win 4 out of a possible 7 games.

Small prizes (certificates, pennants, baseball paraphernalia, etc.) can be presented to the managers of the four teams with the best record. Certificates can be presented to the managers of players that end up as League Leaders in productive, offensive categories. In my classrom. when we got down to the League Championship Series, I had the students play their games in my room during lunch. Each pair of opposing teams mutually agreed upon a student "umpire" to officiate their games (call liners, settle disputes, etc.). When the League Champions had been decided, we moved on to the World Series. Spectators flooded the classroom for both events. League Champions received a pennant of their respective teams while the World Series Champs were awarded tickets to a local professional baseball game.

Teacher Notes

I have found that by starting my year with the Fantasy Baseball unit, I have a great resource for the remainder of the year. Whether it be the day before a vacation or emergency substitute plans, I have something that engages the students and is easy for another teacher to monitor. By allowing the students to return to this at different times throughout the year, they see a purpose for long-term retention of what they have learned. I make it a point to pose questions from time to time that force them to reflect on the experiences they had during the unit; and by referring back to the unit, I can often make connections with new mathematical content being presented to the students.

STUDENT PAGES

and

TRANSPARENCY MASTERS

Name ______________________________

Date ______________________________

Period _______

FANTASY BASEBALL

Pre-Assessment — New Kids In Town

Imagine that two new kids have just moved into your neighborhood and are looking to play on a local baseball or softball team. You have been told by your coach that one of these students will be joining your team. Below are the statistics that they accumulated for their previous teams. Analyze these statistics to help you determine which player you would like to have on your team. On a separate sheet of paper, explain who you would select. Be sure to support your selection with the statistics that are given.

PLAYER A

AB	H	2B	3B	HR	BB	SO
37	13	4	0	5	3	9

PLAYER B

AB	H	2B	3B	HR	BB	SO
61	24	8	3	2	9	7

Which player would you select for your team — Player A? Player B? Explain your reasoning for the player you'd select.

Fantasy Baseball © 1994 by Tim Scheidt

MAJOR LEAGUE BASEBALL TEAMS

NATIONAL LEAGUE

EAST	CENTRAL	WEST
Atlanta Braves	Chicago Cubs	Colorado Rockies
Florida Marlins	Cincinnati Reds	Los Angeles Dodgers
Montreal Expos	Houston Astros	San Diego Padres
New York Mets	Pittsburgh Pirates	San Francisco Giants
Philadelphia Phillies	St. Louis Cardinals	

AMERICAN LEAGUE

EAST	CENTRAL	WEST
Baltimore Orioles	Chicago White Sox	California Angels
Boston Red Sox	Cleveland Indians	Oakland Athletics
Detroit Tigers	Kansas City Royals	Seattle Mariners
New York Yankees	Milwaukee Brewers	Texas Rangers
Toronto Blue Jays	Minnesota Twins	

BASEBALL CARD GLOSSARY

YR — the **year** the player played for a given team.

TEAM — the **team** played for during the year. Major League teams are represented by the team name **(Tigers, Giants, etc.)**. Minor League teams are represented by the city in which the team resides **(Nashville, Eugene, etc.)**

AVG — this number represents the player's **batting average**. This average is the decimal equivalent of the ratio of hits to official at bats.

G — the number of **games** the player appeared in for the team.

AB — this represents the number of **official at bats** the player had during the season. Official at bats (AB) do not include walks (BB) or sacrifice hits (bunts, sacrifice flies). Sacrifice hits do not count as at bats because the player makes an expected out in order to advance the runner(s).

R — the number of **runs** the player scored (times he crossed home plate).

H — the number of **hits** a player got during the season. This number represents the total singles, doubles, triples and home runs the player accumulated during the season.

2B — the number of **doubles** or times the player reached second base safely due to a hit.

3B — the number of **triples** or times the player reached third base safely due to a hit.

HR — the number of **home runs** the player hit during the season.

RBI — the number of **runs batted in** that the player was credited with during the season. This means that other players scored runs due to the player's hitting performance.

BB — the number of **walks** (also known as **bases on balls**) the player received during the season.

SO — the number of **strikeouts** the player had during the season.

SB — the number of **stolen bases** the player had during the season.

Fantasy Baseball © 1994 by Tim Scheidt

FANTASY BASEBALL

Player Guidelines

Use the following guidelines to help you determine whether or not you would like to keep certain players for your team. Although these guidelines do not represent everything you should consider, they'll be helpful when you receive your initial draft of players.

BATTING AVERAGE

below .220 — weak hitter: you won't want to keep unless their other statistics (OB%, HR : Cum. AB ratio, SO : Cum. AB ratio) are considered favorable.

.220 - .250 — low average to average hitter: again, check their other statistics and weigh your choices.

.250 - .300 — good, solid hitter; more than likely you will want to keep a player of this caliber unless their other statistics are unfavorable or you are able to trade for a player with better overall statistics.

.300 & up — excellent hitter: this could be your superstar. Look over the other statistics but expect to keep this player.

ON-BASE PERCENTAGE

The opinion of a group of student experts:

> ***"We like to see a player that has an on-base percentage that is 60 to 100 points higher than their batting average. We also feel that this percentage should be .340 or higher. The higher the percentage, the better!"***

HR : CUM. AB (UNIT) RATIO

The guidelines for this statistic generated by the same group of student experts:

> ***"We consider a HR : Cum. AB ratio of 1:30 to be very good. We feel that this ratio or one that has a smaller number deserves strong consideration. The smaller the number, the better!"***

SO : CUM. AB (UNIT) RATIO

The guidelines for this statistic, also generated by the group of student experts:

> ***"We consider a SO : Cum. AB ratio of 1:8 to be very good. We feel that this ratio or one that has a larger number deserves strong consideration. In this case, the larger the number, the better!"***

FANTASY BASEBALL

Player Comparison Chart

Team Name ______________________________

Managers ______________________ ______________________

Complete the chart below for each of the eligible players you have received. Be sure to calculate the batting average and on-base percentage to the nearest **thousandth** and record the HR:Cum. AB ratio and SO:Cum. AB ratio as unit ratios rounded to the nearest **whole number.**

Pos./YR	Name	AB	Cum. AB	Avg.	OB%	HR : Cum. AB	SO: Cum. AB

Fantasy Baseball © 1994 by Tim Scheidt

Transparency Master

Robin Ventura Card

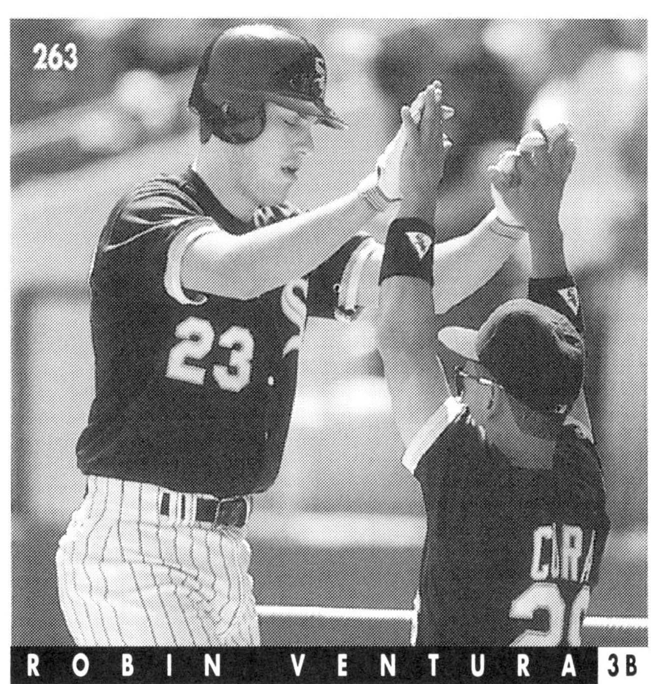

Height: 6'1" **Weight:** 192 lbs. **Bats:** Left **Throws:** Right **Born:** 7-14-67 Santa Maria, California

YR	TEAM	AVG	G	AB	R	H	2B	3B	HR	RBI	BB	SO	SB
89	WHITE SOX	.178	16	45	5	8	3	0	0	7	8	6	0
90	WHITE SOX	.249	150	493	48	123	17	1	5	54	55	53	1
91	WHITE SOX	.284	157	606	92	172	25	1	23	100	80	67	2
92	WHITE SOX	.282	157	592	85	167	38	1	16	93	93	71	2
4	**TOTALS**	.271	480	1736	230	470	83	3	44	254	236	197	5

Ventura won the American League Gold Glove at third base for the second consecutive year

Upper Deck and the card/hologram combination are trademarks of The Upper Deck Company.
© 1992 The Upper Deck Co. All Rights Reserved.
Printed in the U.S.A.

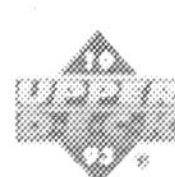

Transparency Master

Activity 1 Manager's Log

Describe the best player you feel you received in the initial draft. Use the statistical information you gathered to support your selection.

Activity 2 Manager's Log

Write a letter describing your team to a real Major League team's manager (Sparky Anderson, Tommy Lasorda, etc.) What are your team's strengths? What are its weaknesses? Do you feel your team will be competitive during the season? Why or why not? Be creative with your writing!

Activity 3 Manager's Log

Explain the process you used to complete a thorough statistical analysis of the players on your team. How can you tell whether or not your analysis is accurate?

Fantasy Baseball © 1994 by Tim Scheidt

Transparency Master

Activity 1 Performance Assessment

Calculate the batting average, on-base percentage, HR : Cum. AB ratio and SO : Cum. AB ratio for each player. Include a written analysis of both players.

Activity 3 Performance Assessment

Analyze the statistics for each player just like you did for the players on your teams. Write a summary of the process you use to do this analysis.

Activity 5 Performance Assessment

Create a new Pitcher Batting Guide that increases the likelihood of favorable outcomes, yet is reasonable. Record the ratios and percentages for hits : possible outcomes, on base : possible outcomes and outs : possible outcomes. Write a description of the process you use to create this new guide.

Transparency Master

Activity 2 Discussion Questions

(The Draft — What Are Our Chances?)

What is the probability of getting the first player selected in the draft? How did you determine this?

Is this probability the same for all teams? Why or why not?

If one of your cards is selected first, does the probability increase or decrease for having your second card selected? Explain your reasoning.

Do you think this lottery method is a fair way for conducting the free agent draft? If so, explain why you think it is fair. If not, why isn't it fair and what would you change to make it fair?

Fantasy Baseball © 1994 by Tim Scheidt

FANTASY BASEBALL

Statistical Guide

This guide is intended to be used as a resource as you complete the **Player Analysis Chart** for each of your players. You will find all of the statistics you will need to complete the charts on the back of your baseball cards.

* To find **cumulative at-bats (Cum. AB)** — add the number of at-bats (AB) to the number of bases on ball (BB) shown on the card.

* To find **singles (1B)** — subtract the number of doubles (2B), triples (3B) and home runs (HR) from the number of hits (H) shown on the card.

* To determine **Other Outs** — add the hits (H), bases on balls (BB) and strike outs (SO) and subtract the total from the **Cum. AB**.

* To determine **Fly Outs (FO)** and **Ground Outs (GO)** — divide the number of **Other Outs** by 2. The quotient goes under each heading **(FO)** and **(GO)**.

Example:	**Other Outs**	**142**	**FO**	**GO**
	142	**2**	**71**	**71**

(If Other Outs yields an odd number, increase either Fly Outs or Ground Outs by 1.)

* To represent the **Ratio of a Statistic to Cum. AB** as a fraction — record the Cum. AB total as the denominator and the value of each statistic as the numerator.

* To determine the **Decimal Equivalent** — divide the numerator by the denominator. Record only to the fourth (4th) decimal place.

Example: $\frac{\text{1B}}{\text{Cum. AB}} = \frac{109}{551} = .1978$

* To determine the **Degrees** — multiply the decimal equivalent for each statistic by **360** (number of degrees in a circle). Round each product to the nearest whole number.

Example: .1978 x 360 = 71.208 or 71 degrees

FANTASY BASEBALL

Player Analysis Chart

(Examples)

YEAR 1991

Name	Cum. AB	H	1B	2B	3B	HR	BB	SO	Other Outs	FO	GO
Robin Ventura	686	172	123	25	1	23	80	67	367	183	184
RATIO			123/686	25/686	1/686	23/686	80/686	67/686		183/686	184/686
DECIMAL EQUIVALENT			.1793	.0364	.0014	.0335	.1166	.0976		.2667	.2682
DEGREES			65°	13°	0°	12°	42°	35°		96°	97°

YEAR 1985

Name	Cum. AB	H	1B	2B	3B	HR	BB	SO	Other Outs	FO	GO
Willie McGee	646	216	162	26	18	10	34	86	310	155	155
RATIO			162/646	26/646	18/646	10/646	34/646	86/646		155/646	155/646
DECIMAL EQUIVALENT			.2508	.0402	.0279	.0155	.0526	.1331		.2399	.2399
DEGREES			90°	14°	10°	6°	19°	48°		86°	86°

Fantasy Baseball © 1994 by Tim Scheidt

FANTASY BASEBALL

Player Analysis Chart

YEAR__________

Name	Cum. AB	H	1B	2B	3B	HR	BB	SO	Other Outs	FO	GO
RATIO											
DECIMAL EQUIVALENT											
DEGREES											

YEAR__________

Name	Cum. AB	H	1B	2B	3B	HR	BB	SO	Other Outs	FO	GO
RATIO											
DECIMAL EQUIVALENT											
DEGREES											

Name ______________________________

Date ______________________________

Period _______

CHALLENGE PROBLEM #1

Catch Him If You Can!

Speed Durgan has frequently been clocked at 3.4 seconds running the ninety (90) feet from one base to another. Bull McKinley, pitcher, throws a fastball consistently at 84 m.p.h. Rich Crowe, catcher, has been clocked at 70 m.p.h. throwing the ball from homeplate to second base. It normally takes Rich 1.3 seconds to release the ball once he has caught it from Bull.

If Speed has a 3-foot lead at first base and heads for second base at precisely the same time that Bull releases the ball, will Speed be safe or out? Support your conclusion with your calculations and any other factors you believe warrant consideration.

*** The distance from the pitcher's mound to home plate is 60'6".**

Fantasy Baseball © 1994 by Tim Scheidt

FANTASY BASEBALL

Problem of the Week (P.O.W.) Procedure

Use the following P.O.W. procedure to find a solution to the Challenge Problems. Record your information on a separate sheet of paper.

1. **STATE THE PROBLEM.** Write this in a complete sentence or sentences. Also, describe the initial strategy you plan to use for working with the problem.

2. **DO THE WORK.** Include pictures, calculations, charts, equations, etc. — whatever you find to be useful to arrive at a solution.

3. **STATE YOUR SOLUTION.** Write this in a complete sentence or sentences.

4. **EXPLAIN YOUR REASONING.** In a complete paragraph or paragraphs, explain why you believe your solution to be a reasonable one. Be sure to refer to your work (#2) when justifying the reasonableness of your solution.

Transparency Master

Activity 3 Discussion Questions

(How Can We Use These Player Statistics?)

What statistical information that is present on the wheels is also present on the baseball cards? What information on the wheels is not on the cards? How could you get this information?

Using data from the cards, how can you determine how many times a player has been up to bat? [Remember, BB's are not included in the AB's on the cards.] How would knowing this help you with constructing your wheels?

How could you represent each statistic on the baseball cards as a fraction? What would each statistic be a fraction of?

Could you use these fractions to get the information you need in order to construct the wheels? How can you find the decimal and/or percentage equivalent of these fractions? How could this information be helpful?

What is the relationship between percentages and fractions? What would the denominator of a fractional representation of 17% be?

What unit of measure is used for measuring circles? Is this important to know to make your wheels statistically accurate? Why or why not?

How precise do you think you need to be in your calculations? Why is a certain level of precision important?

Fantasy Baseball © 1994 by Tim Scheidt

FANTASY BASEBALL

How To Make A Player Wheel

YEAR 1991

Name	Cum. AB	H	1B	2B	3B	HR	BB	SO	Other Outs	FO	GO
Robin Ventura	686	172	123	25	1	23	80	67	367	183	184
RATIO			$\frac{123}{686}$	$\frac{25}{686}$	$\frac{1}{686}$	$\frac{23}{686}$	$\frac{80}{686}$	$\frac{67}{686}$		$\frac{183}{686}$	$\frac{184}{686}$
DECIMAL EQUIVALENT			.1793	.0364	.0014	.0335	.1166	.0976		.2667	.2682
DEGREES			65°	13°	0°	12°	42°	35°		96°	97°

A. Use a copy of the **Player Wheel** master or construct two (2) circles, $4\frac{1}{2}$" in diameter, on cardstock. Clearly mark the center point on the circles.

B. Using your protractor as a straight edge, draw a radius anywhere in your wheel.

C. Get out your completed **Player Analysis Charts.** Determine your preferred order of placement for each statistical category. Using your first category, construct the appropriate angle and draw another radius. Label this section of your wheel with the correct statistical abbreviation.

D. Continue **Step C** until all of the angles have been measured and the statistical abbreviations recorded on the wheel.

E. Write the player's full name on the back of the wheel.

F. Cut out the player wheel.

G. Cut a blank sheet of cardstock (different color) width-wise into 2 equal pieces. These serve as the wheel base.

H.
- If you are going to use transparent spinners, center your wheel and glue stick it on to a blank base.
- If you are going to make spinners out of the wheels, follow the **Making Spinners** directions that follow.

I. Decorate the base of your player wheels. Be creative! Be sure to include the player's name, position, team name and current batting average, somewhere on the base.

FANTASY BASEBALL

How To Make A Player Wheel

(pictorial model)

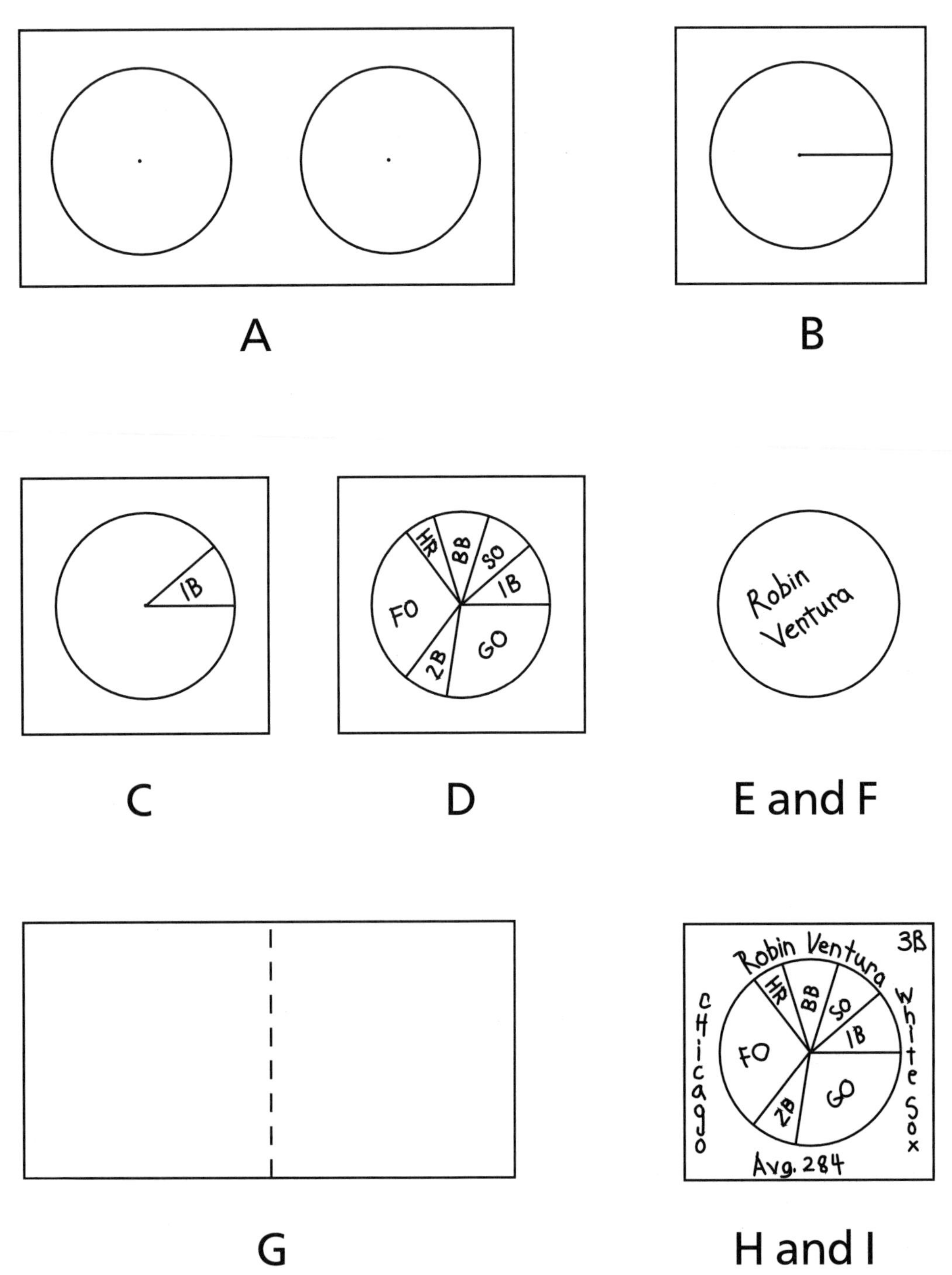

Fantasy Baseball © 1994 by Tim Scheidt

FANTASY BASEBALL

Making Spinners

1. Estimate the center of the base. lightly mark a point at the center. Using a straight edge, draw a dark, thin line from the center point to the lower left corner.

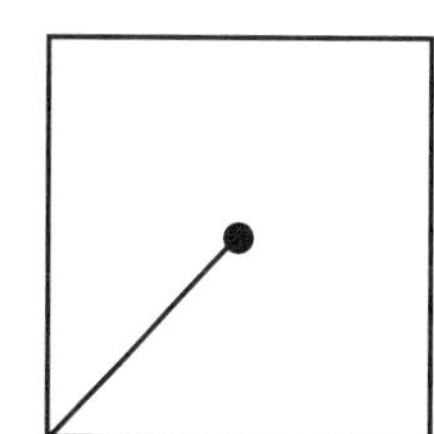

2. Cut out three 1" by 1" squares from the paper scraps left from cutting out the wheels.

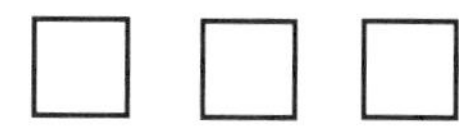

3. Bend your paper clip so that the smaller, inside loop bends up. Pull the end of the this loop up to expose the pointed end. Use this point to poke holes in the center of the wheel and center point of the base.

4. Put bent paper clip through the center hole of the base (clip goes up through the bottom). The large loop of the paper clip should lay flat along the bottom of the base.

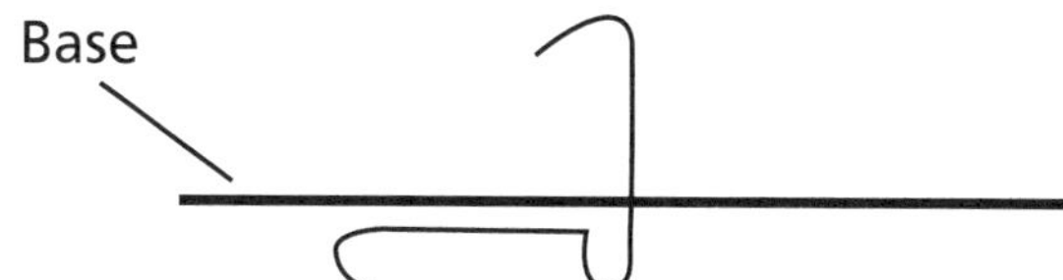

5. Place your three paper squares (washers) and then your wheel over the paper clip and on top of the base. Bend the paper clip down.

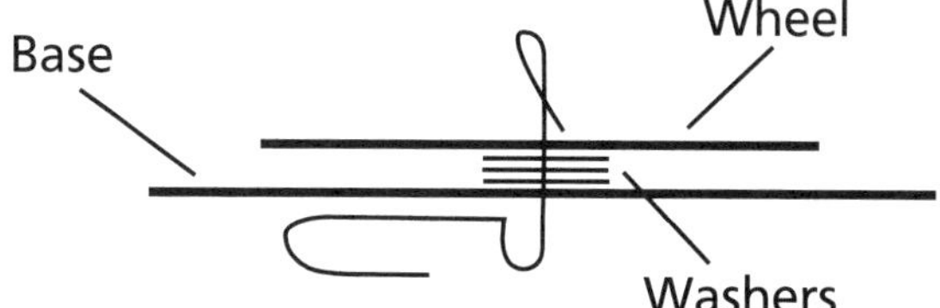

6. Put masking tape on the bottom to hold the paper clip flush against the base.

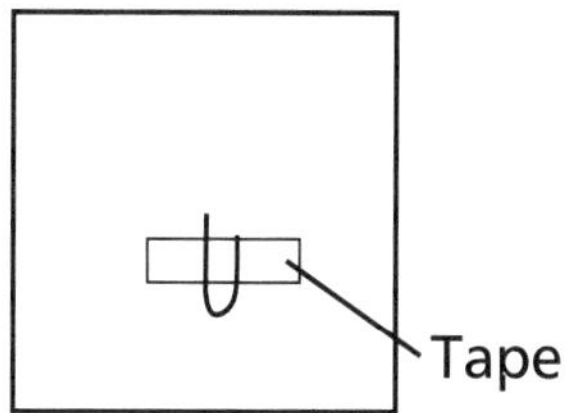

PLAYER WHEEL MASTER

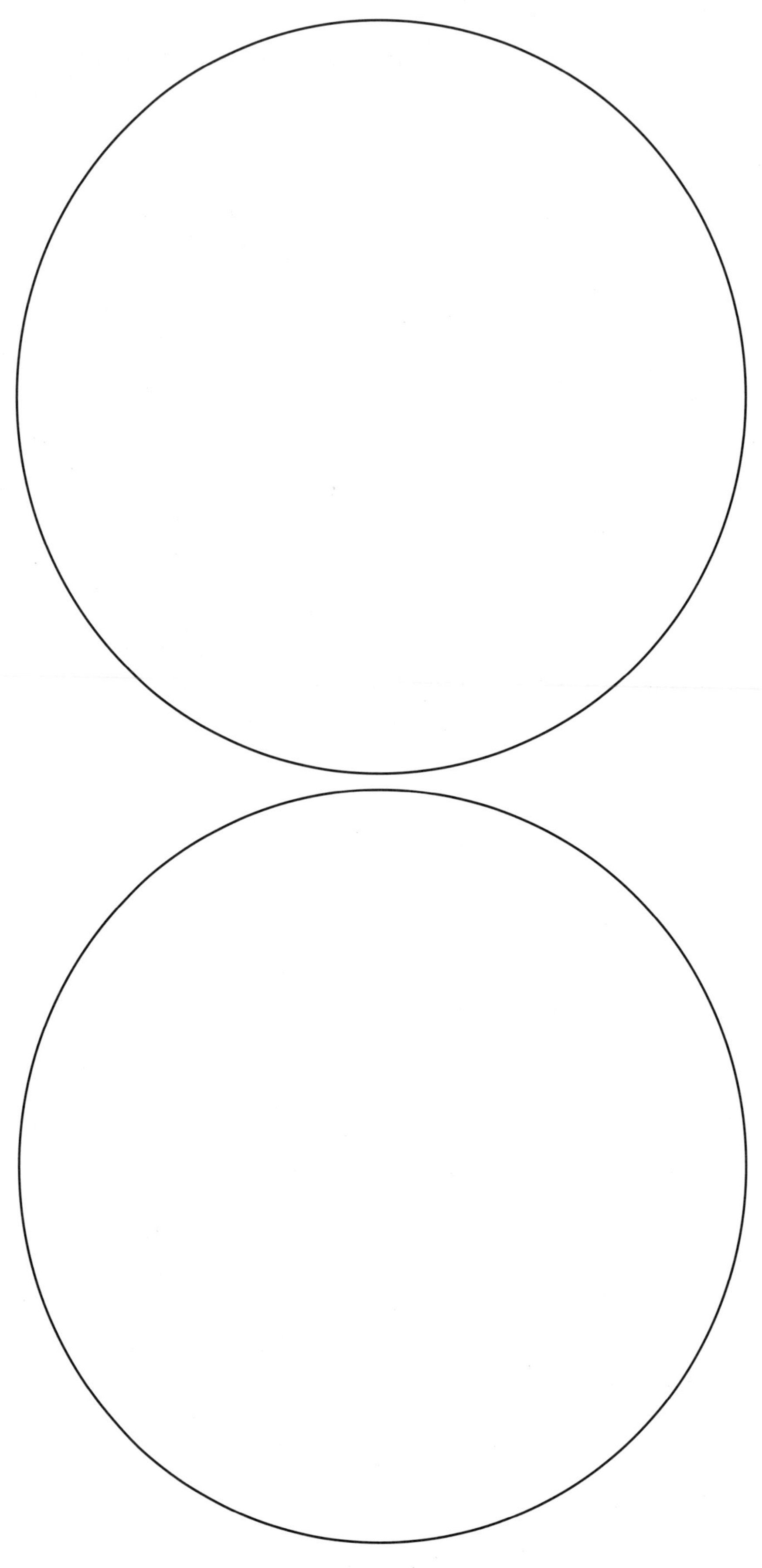

Fantasy Baseball © 1994 by Tim Scheidt

Transparency Master

Activity 4 Manager's Log

My impression of Fantasy Baseball, so far . . .

Activity 5 Manager's Log

Describe what you discovered during your investigation of the Pitcher Batting Guide. How will this information be of use to you when playing actual games?

Activity 6 Manager's Log

In a few days you will be playing your first game of the regular season. Write a letter to the General Manager (GM) of your team. List the batting order you plan to use for that first game. Justify your placement of the players in this order by referring to any key statistical measures that have influenced your decisions.

FANTASY BASEBALL

Scorekeeping Guide

This guide is to be used to answer scoring questions that may come up during the course of a game. This guide does not attempt to reflect individual situations that arise in a real game, but rather provides a consistent standard to be applied in all Fantasy Baseball games.

IF THE PERSON UP TO BAT GETS A . . .	THE RUNNERS ON BASE . . .
• Single (1B)	advance one base.
• Double (2B)	advance two bases.
• Triple (3B)	all score.
• Homerun (HR)	all score.
• Base on Balls (BB)	advance one base only if they are forced to as a result of the batter being awarded first base.
• Strikeout (SO)	do not advance.
• Fly Out (FO)	do not advance unless there is a runner on third base with less than two outs. If this is the case, the runner on third scores on the out.
• Ground Out (GO)	advance one base unless there are two outs in the inning.

Fantasy Baseball © 1994 by Tim Scheidt

FANTASY BASEBALL

Pitcher Batting Guide

When it is time for your pitcher to bat, you will be using dice as your pitchers do not have player wheels. Below you will find the scoring possibilities for each possible sum of the two dice. Record your pitcher's batting record just the way you would with your other players.

IF YOU ROLL A . . .	YOUR PITCHER GETS A . . .
2	double (2B)
3	single (1B)
4	strikeout (SO)
5	base on balls (BB)
6	fly out (FO)
7	strikeout (SO)
8	ground out (GO)
9	strikeout (SO)
10	fly out (FO)
11	single (1B)
12	homerun (HR)

Scoresheet

_______________ VS _______________ AT _______________ SCORER _______________ DATE _______________

Score by Inning	1	2	3	4	5	6	7	8	9	10

Final Score	

Name	POS	1	2	3	4	5	6	7	8	9	10	AB	R	H	2B	3B	HR	BB	SO	RBI
		BB 1B 2B 3B HR	BB 1B 2B 3B HR	BB 1B 2B 3B HR	BB 1B 2B 3B HR	BB 1B 2B 3B HR	BB 1B 2B 3B HR	BB 1B 2B 3B HR	BB 1B 2B 3B HR	BB 1B 2B 3B HR	BB 1B 2B 3B HR									
		BB 1B 2B 3B HR	BB 1B 2B 3B HR	BB 1B 2B 3B HR	BB 1B 2B 3B HR	BB 1B 2B 3B HR	BB 1B 2B 3B HR	BB 1B 2B 3B HR	BB 1B 2B 3B HR	BB 1B 2B 3B HR	BB 1B 2B 3B HR									
		BB 1B 2B 3B HR	BB 1B 2B 3B HR	BB 1B 2B 3B HR	BB 1B 2B 3B HR	BB 1B 2B 3B HR	BB 1B 2B 3B HR	BB 1B 2B 3B HR	BB 1B 2B 3B HR	BB 1B 2B 3B HR	BB 1B 2B 3B HR									
		BB 1B 2B 3B HR	BB 1B 2B 3B HR	BB 1B 2B 3B HR	BB 1B 2B 3B HR	BB 1B 2B 3B HR	BB 1B 2B 3B HR	BB 1B 2B 3B HR	BB 1B 2B 3B HR	BB 1B 2B 3B HR	BB 1B 2B 3B HR									
		BB 1B 2B 3B HR	BB 1B 2B 3B HR	BB 1B 2B 3B HR	BB 1B 2B 3B HR	BB 1B 2B 3B HR	BB 1B 2B 3B HR	BB 1B 2B 3B HR	BB 1B 2B 3B HR	BB 1B 2B 3B HR	BB 1B 2B 3B HR									
		BB 1B 2B 3B HR	BB 1B 2B 3B HR	BB 1B 2B 3B HR	BB 1B 2B 3B HR	BB 1B 2B 3B HR	BB 1B 2B 3B HR	BB 1B 2B 3B HR	BB 1B 2B 3B HR	BB 1B 2B 3B HR	BB 1B 2B 3B HR									
		BB 1B 2B 3B HR	BB 1B 2B 3B HR	BB 1B 2B 3B HR	BB 1B 2B 3B HR	BB 1B 2B 3B HR	BB 1B 2B 3B HR	BB 1B 2B 3B HR	BB 1B 2B 3B HR	BB 1B 2B 3B HR	BB 1B 2B 3B HR									
		BB 1B 2B 3B HR	BB 1B 2B 3B HR	BB 1B 2B 3B HR	BB 1B 2B 3B HR	BB 1B 2B 3B HR	BB 1B 2B 3B HR	BB 1B 2B 3B HR	BB 1B 2B 3B HR	BB 1B 2B 3B HR	BB 1B 2B 3B HR									
		BB 1B 2B 3B HR	BB 1B 2B 3B HR	BB 1B 2B 3B HR	BB 1B 2B 3B HR	BB 1B 2B 3B HR	BB 1B 2B 3B HR	BB 1B 2B 3B HR	BB 1B 2B 3B HR	BB 1B 2B 3B HR	BB 1B 2B 3B HR									
		BB 1B 2B 3B HR	BB 1B 2B 3B HR	BB 1B 2B 3B HR	BB 1B 2B 3B HR	BB 1B 2B 3B HR	BB 1B 2B 3B HR	BB 1B 2B 3B HR	BB 1B 2B 3B HR	BB 1B 2B 3B HR	BB 1B 2B 3B HR									
Team Totals																				

Fantasy Baseball © 1994 by Tim Scheidt

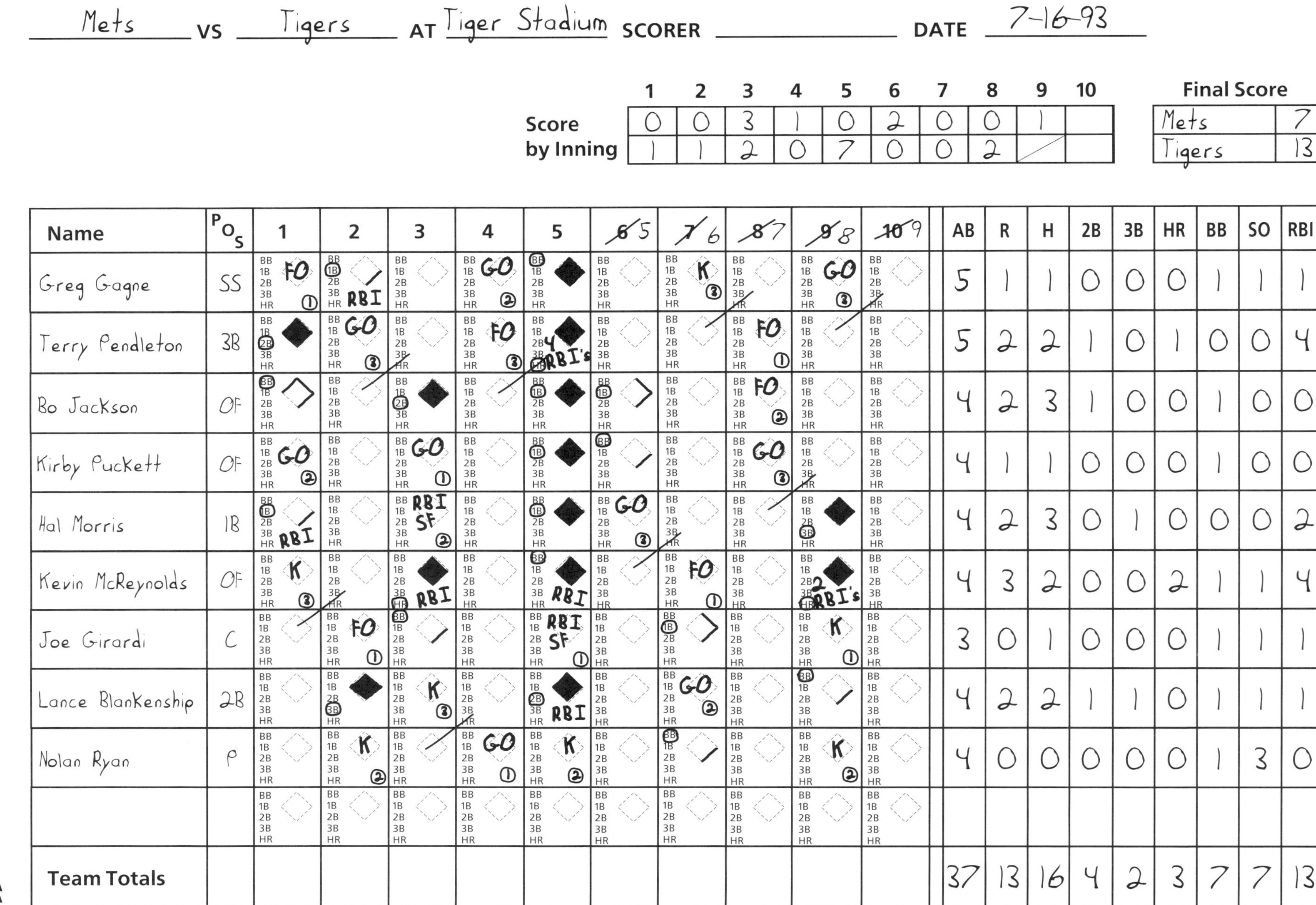

Sample Scoresheet

Mets VS Tigers AT Tiger Stadium SCORER ______ DATE 7-16-93

Score by Inning

	1	2	3	4	5	6	7	8	9	10
Mets	0	0	3	1	0	2	0	0	1	
Tigers	1	1	2	0	7	0	0	2	/	

Final Score

Mets	7
Tigers	13

Name	Pos	1	2	3	4	5	~~6~~ 5	~~7~~ 6	~~8~~ 7	~~9~~ 8	~~10~~ 9
Greg Gagne	SS	FO ①	1B RBI		GO ②	BB ◆		K ③		GO ③	
Terry Pendleton	3B	2B ◆	GO ③		FO ③	HR ◆ 4 RBI's			FO ①		
Bo Jackson	OF	BB		2B ◆		1B ◆	1B		FO ②		
Kirby Puckett	OF	GO ②		GO ①		1B ◆	BB		GO ③		
Hal Morris	1B	1B RBI		RBI SF ②		1B ◆	GO ③			3B ◆	
Kevin McReynolds	OF	K ③		HR ◆ RBI		BB ◆ RBI		FO ①		HR ◆ 2 RBI's	
Joe Girardi	C		FO ①	BB		RBI SF ①		1B		K ①	
Lance Blankenship	2B		3B ◆	K ③		2B ◆ RBI		GO ②		BB	
Nolan Ryan	P		K ②		GO ①	K ②		BB		K ②	
Team Totals											

Name	AB	R	H	2B	3B	HR	BB	SO	RBI
Greg Gagne	5	1	1	0	0	0	1	1	1
Terry Pendleton	5	2	2	1	0	1	0	0	4
Bo Jackson	4	2	3	1	0	0	1	0	0
Kirby Puckett	4	1	1	0	0	0	1	0	0
Hal Morris	4	2	3	0	1	0	0	0	2
Kevin McReynolds	4	3	2	0	0	2	1	1	4
Joe Girardi	3	0	1	0	0	0	1	1	1
Lance Blankenship	4	2	2	1	1	0	1	1	1
Nolan Ryan	4	0	0	0	0	0	1	3	0
Team Totals	37	13	16	4	2	3	7	7	13

Transparency Master

Activity 5 Discussion Questions

(Investigating the Pitcher Batting Guide)

What is the ratio of chances of getting a hit to possible outcomes? What percentage of possible outcomes is this?

What is the ratio of chances of reaching base to possible outcomes? What percentage of possible outcomes is this?

What is the ratio of chances of getting out to possible outcomes? What percentage of possible outcomes is this?

Do these three percentages total 100%? Why or why not?

Do you think the pitcher has a good chance of getting on base? Why or why not?

Fantasy Baseball © 1994 by Tim Scheidt

Name ______________________________

Date ______________________________

Period _______

CHALLENGE PROBLEM #2

Flashy Uniforms

To promote attendance at your team's upcoming games, you have decided to furnish your players with outlandish uniforms. You believe that the flashier the uniforms, the greater the fan interest. The problem is, how will you decide on which color combination to use for your new uniforms?

You know that you need to purchase the following articles for your players:

jersey, pants, stirrups, shoes and a **hat.**

The following colors are available for your uniforms:

black, white, peach, teal, red, blue and **orange.**

In order to stay within league guidelines, you must adhere to the following:

- Your jerseys must consist of **three** different colors
- Your pants must consist of **two** different colors
- Your stirrups must be **one** solid color
- Your shoes must consist of **two** different colors with the laces being of a different color than those of the shoes
- Your hat must consist of **three** different colors

How many different color combinations are possible for a complete uniform if you follow the league guidelines stated above?

** Design and draw a uniform for your team using one of the possible combinations.

FANTASY BASEBALL

Team Stat Sheet

Manager ______________________ Manager ______________________

Team ______________________

Name	AB	R	H	2B	3B	HR	BB	SO	RBI	AVG.	OB%	SLG.%

Fantasy Baseball © 1994 by Tim Scheidt

FANTASY BASEBALL

Sample Schedules

MONDAY	TUESDAY	WEDNESDAY
Yankees vs. Padres	Yankees vs. Phillies	Yankees vs. Tigers
Tigers vs. Giants	Tigers vs. Mets	Orioles vs. Angels
Angels vs. Phillies	Angels vs. Padres	Padres vs. Giants
Orioles vs. Mets	Orioles vs. Giants	Phillies vs. Mets
Yankees vs. Giants	Yankees vs. Mets	Yankees vs. Angels
Tigers vs. Phillies	Tigers vs. Padres	Orioles vs. Tigers
Angels vs. Mets	Angels vs. Giants	Phillies vs. Padres
Orioles vs. Padres	Orioles vs. Phillies	Giants vs. Mets

- -

MONDAY	TUESDAY	WEDNESDAY	NUMBERS/TEAMS
1 vs. 8	1 vs. 6	1 vs. 4	1 - Yankees
2 vs. 7	2 vs. 5	2 vs. 3	2 - Tigers
3 vs. 6	3 vs. 8	5 vs. 8	3 - Angels
4 vs. 5	4 vs. 7	6 vs. 7	4 - Orioles
			5 - Padres
1 vs. 7	1 vs. 5	1 vs. 3	6 - Giants
2 vs. 6	2 vs. 8	2 vs. 4	7 - Phillies
3 vs. 5	3 vs. 7	5 vs. 7	8 - Mets
4 vs. 8	4 vs. 6	6 vs. 8	

FANTASY BASEBALL

Assignment — Regular Season Schedule

Work with your partner to create a ten-day **Fantasy Baseball Regular Season Schedule** that may possibly be used by your class. Your schedule must be easy to read and include the following:

- Each team must play every other team at least once.
- Each team must play twenty (20) games.
- Each team must have an equitable number of home games.

Design your schedule around the ten class periods that your teacher designates to you as Fantasy Baseball game days. Remember, each team should be scheduled for two games per day.

If you have an odd number of teams in your class, one team will receive what is called a "bye" during each round of games. When a team has a "bye" they play the game with only their team and automatically get credited with a win. No team should get more than two "byes" on your schedule.

***** SPECIAL NOTE: Those that creatively copy their finished schedule onto a large posterboard will be eligible to have their schedule included in the voting for the Fantasy Baseball Schedule to be used by the class.**

Fantasy Baseball © 1994 by Tim Scheidt

Transparency Master

Activity 6 Discussion Questions

(Player Placement — Does It Really Matter?)

Look at your Team Stat Sheet. Do all of your players have the same number of at-bats? Which players tend to have more, those that are placed at the beginning of the lineup or those placed at the end? Is there a significant difference? According to their statistics, are there certain players you would want to have bat more than others?

Where in your lineup do you want to place a player that has a high batting average? How about a player with a high on-base %? How would their order possibly make a difference in a game?

Where would be a good spot for a player that has a tendency to hit a lot of home runs? Why would this spot possibly be a productive one?

How do your pitchers' statistics compare with those of your other players? If they are significantly lower, why do you think this is so? If they are comparable, do you feel they should always bat last in your lineup? Why or why not?

Fantasy Baseball © 1994 by Tim Scheidt

Transparency Master

Activity 6 Discussion Questions

(A Return to Looking at Player Placement)

On your Team Stat Sheet you have three very important statistical measures: average (Avg.), on-base percentage (OB%), and slugging percentage (SLG. %). Make a list for each measure, placing the player with the highest mark at the top of the list and proceeding in numerical order. Are your players consistently in the same spot for all measures or does their placement vary from measure to measure?

Where in your lineup do you want to place a player that has a high slugging average? How would the placement of this player possibly make a difference in a game?

Do you feel these statistics for 5 games are an accurate measure of what your players will do over the course of a 40–50 game season? Why or why not? Is there any other data you may want to consider when ordering the players in your lineup? If so, where will you get it?

Fantasy Baseball © 1994 by Tim Scheidt

Transparency Master

Activity 6 Performance Assessment

Where in your batting order would you place these players? Use statistical data to support your decisions.

Activity 8 Performance Assessment

Respond to the following situation using writing, diagrams, charts, wheels, etc., — anything that will help you to convey your reasoning:

> *You are in the bottom of the ninth inning of a 3 to 3 ball game. You have runners on first and third with two outs and your pitcher is up to bat. You have two choices — let your pitcher bat or have the runner on third (which happens to be your second baseman) attempt to steal home. What will you do? Support your decision with strong mathematical reasoning.*

Fantasy Baseball © 1994 by Tim Scheidt

Name ______________________________

Date ______________________________

Period _______

FANTASY BASEBALL

Theoretical vs. Experimental Probability

What should happen (theoretical) . . .

Name	Cum. AB	H	1B	2B	3B	HR	BB	SO	FO	GO
RATIO										
DECIMAL EQUIVALENT										
PERCENTAGE										
THEORETICAL PROBABILITY (360 SPINS)										

My prediction for 360 spins . . .

Name	Cum. AB	H	1B	2B	3B	HR	BB	SO	FO	GO
	360									

Results of 360 spins (experimental) . . .

Name	Cum. AB	H	1B	2B	3B	HR	BB	SO	FO	GO
	360									

Fantasy Baseball © 1994 by Tim Scheidt

Transparency Master

Activity 7 Manager's Log

In your own words, explain what you have done in class these past few days and what you have learned. Be sure to include as much as possible regarding what you've learned about probability.

Activity 8 Manager's Log

Write a short newspaper article that provides an update on what has happened with your baseball team. What is your record? How are individual players doing? Have you, as co-manager, made any recent decisions that have helped the team? What is the outlook for the next five games?

Unit Wrap Manager's Log

Write a paragraph or two on each of your three players, comparing the statistics on their baseball cards with the statistics you gathered during the regular season. Use your completed charts as tools to provide an accurate comparison of these statistics.

FANTASY BASEBALL

Team Standings/Avg. Leaders

(Examples)

FANTASY BASEBALL

TEAM STANDINGS

American League				National League			
TEAM	W	L	PCT.	TEAM	W	L	PCT.
Tigers	5	0	1.000	Cardinals	4	1	.800
Orioles	4	1	.800	Padres	4	1	.800
Twins	4	1	.800	Giants	3	2	.600
Royals	3	2	.600	Expos	2	3	.400
Yankees	3	2	.600	Mets	1	4	.200
Indians	2	3	.400	Cubs	0	5	.000
Rangers	0	5	.000	Dodgers	0	5	.000

FANTASY BASEBALL

BATTING AVERAGE LEADERS

NAME	TEAM	AVERAGE
Lou Whitaker	Tigers	.583
Will Clark	Mets	.514
Wade Boggs	Indians	.474
Frank Thomas	Twins	.459
Andre Dawson	Giants	.406
Barry Bonds	Cardinals	.388
Ken Griffey Jr.	Cardinals	.372
Gary Sheffield	Orioles	.351
Tony Gwynn	Rangers	.349
Paul Molitor	Padres	.333

Fantasy Baseball © 1994 by Tim Scheidt

Name ______________________________

Date ______________________________

Period _______

CHALLENGE PROBLEM #3

Salary Hike 2000

In 1981, Dave Winfield of the New York Yankees received a record contract that paid him 2.2 million dollars per year. In 1992, Ryne Sandberg of the Chicago Cubs signed a record-breaking contract that guaranteed him an average salary of 7.1 million dollars per year.

Use what you know about growth to do the following:

- Find the growth factor for the add-on model of growth and the multiply-by model of growth for these salaries. Use these respective growth factors to predict what the potential top salary could be in the year 2000.

- Write a letter to the Commissioner of Baseball either supporting or opposing these salary increases. Be sure to refer to your mathematical predictions in your letter.

Transparency Master

Activity 8 Discussion Questions

(After 5 Games — Investigating Stolen Bases)

Are all base runners equally adept at stealing bases?

Should everyone have the same chances of success?

Are some bases easier to steal than others?

Can more than one runner steal a base at a time?

Can a runner steal more than one base at a time?

Are there any bases that can't be stolen?

Are there any situations where a runner cannot steal a base?

How can we use the information on the baseball cards to help us create our method?

Fantasy Baseball © 1994 by Tim Scheidt

Transparency Master

Unit Wrap Discussion Questions

(Activity Wrap — Manager's Log)

If you were to begin a new Fantasy Baseball season, would you keep your current player wheels or make new ones based on their new statistics? Explain your choice.

Do you think your players would have better or worse statistics if they were to play 25 more games? Explain your reasoning.

After playing 20 regular season games of Fantasy Baseball, do you feel that the placement of statistical categories had any impace on the results? Why or why not?

Would you do anything differently regarding placement of statistics if you had to create new player wheels? If so, what would you do?

Name ______________________________

Date ______________________________

Period _______

INDIVIDUAL ASSESSMENT

Free Agent Deal

Two new players have just been made available for the Free Agent Draft of Fantasy Baseball. Below you will find the statistics from their most recent years of service. Analyze these statistics so that you can determine which player you would select for your team. Be sure to support your selection with statistical data.

PLAYER A

AB	H	2B	3B	HR	BB	SO
489	161	31	3	7	97	48

PLAYER B

AB	H	2B	3B	HR	BB	SO
619	186	42	2	32	87	114

Who would you draft: Player A? Player B? Why?

Fantasy Baseball © 1994 by Tim Scheidt

FANTASY BASEBALL PROJECT

An Open-Ended Assessment

Situation:
You and your partner have just been hired as consultants for a major publishing firm. They have heard about a math unit called **Fantasy Baseball** and are seeking your help to learn more about the unit. If they consider the unit to be worthwhile, they intend to publish and market it under the company name. The publishing firm has two major concerns:

1. They want to be sure that the unit contains plenty of mathematics suitable for the students that participate in the unit.

2. They want to be sure that students are given the opportunity to communicate with others and use their creativity while participating in the unit.

Remember, the publisher knows very little about the unit — this is why you have been hired on by the firm.

Your Task
Create a display that explains what the **Fantasy Baseball** unit is all about. This display should include samples, illustrations, written descriptions, etc. — anything that will help the publisher get a clear picture of the unit. Be sure to give a great deal of consideration to the two concerns mentioned above. You may wish to gather additional information about your own **Fantasy Baseball** team to help with designing your display.

Be prepared to give a 3–5 minute presentation to the Board of Directors, providing them with the information they need to make a decision on whether or not to publish this unit. You will be evaluated by the Board on the clarity of your presentation, along with your visual and written display.

Manager(s): ______________________ ______________________

FANTASY BASEBALL PROJECT
Board Comments

Presentation: ______________________

____

____

____

Display: ______________________

____

____

____

- -

Manager(s): ______________________ ______________________

FANTASY BASEBALL PROJECT
Board Comments

Presentation: ______________________

____

____

____

Display: ______________________

____

____

____

Fantasy Baseball © 1994 by Tim Scheidt

PÁGINAS ESTUDIANTILES

Y

TRANSPARENCIAS

Nombre ____________________________________

Fecha ______________________________________

Período __________________

BÉISBOL DE FANTASÍA

Pre-Evaluación — Los nuevos chicos del pueblo

Imagínate que dos nuevos chicos han llegado a tu vecindario y buscan un equipo local para jugar béisbol. El entrenador te dijo que uno de ellos entrará a tu equipo. Abajo se encuentran las estadísticas que ellos acumularon para sus equipos previos. Analiza estas estadísticas para determinar cuál de los dos jugadores querrías tener en tu equipo. En otra hoja de papel, escribe que jugador preferirías para tu equipo y explica porqué. Confirma tu selección con las estadísticas facilitadas.

JUGADOR A

AB	H	2B	3B	HR	BB	SO
37	13	4	0	5	3	9

JUGADOR B

AB	H	2B	3B	HR	BB	SO
61	24	8	3	2	9	7

¿Qué jugador prefieres para tu equipo — ¿El jugador A? o ¿El jugador B? Explica tu Elección.

Fantasy Baseball © 1994 by Tim Scheidt

LOS EQUIPOS DE LAS LIGAS MAYORES DE BÉISBOL

LIGA NACIONAL

ESTE	CENTRAL	OESTE
Atlanta Braves	Chicago Cubs	Colorado Rockies
Florida Marlins	Cincinnati Reds	Los Angeles Dodgers
Montreal Expos	Houston Astros	San Diego Padres
New York Mets	Pittsburgh Pirates	San Francisco Giants
Philadelphia Phillies	St. Louis Cardinals	

LIGA NORTEAMERICANA

ESTE	CENTRAL	OESTE
Baltimore Orioles	Chicago White Sox	California Angels
Boston Red Sox	Cleveland Indians	Oakland Athletics
Detroit Tigers	Kansas City Royals	Seattle Mariners
New York Yankees	Milwaukee Brewers	Texas Rangers
Toronto Blue Jays	Minnesota Twins	

Glosario de las tarjetas de béisbol

YR — El **año** en que el beisbolista jugó para el equipo nombrado.

TEAM — El **equipo** para el que jugó durante el año. Los equipos de la liga mayor se representan por el nombre del equipo **(Tigers, Giants, etc.)**. Los equipos de la liga menor se representan por el nombre de la ciudad en que residen **(Nashville, Eugene, etc.)**.

AVG — Este número representa el **promedio de batear**, o sea las veces que llega a base con un tiro sencillo, doble, triple, o un jonrón.

G — El número de **partidos** que el jugador jugó para el equipo durante la temporada.

AB — El número **oficial de batear** que el jugador obtuvo durante la temporada. (AB) no incluye las veces que llegó a la base por bolas (BB) o los sacrificios. Los sacrificios no se cuentan porque el bateador tira intencionadamente la bola fuera para que su compañero pueda llegar a la base.

R — El número de **carreras** (las veces que pasa al jon).

H — El número de **tiros** que llegan a la base. Este número representa los tiros sencillos, dobles, triples y jonrónes que hizo el jugador durante la temporada.

2B — El número de **dobles** que hizo, o sea las veces que llegó a la segunda base con solo un tiro.

3B — La cantidad de **veces** que hizo un triple o que llegó a la tercera base con solo un tiro.

HR — El número **jonrones** que hizo durante la temporada.

RBI — El número de carreras que pueden hacer sus compañeros gracias a sus tiros.

BB — El número de **bases por bolas** durante la temporada.

SO — El número de **ponchadas**.

SB — El número **bases que roba** un jugador durante la temporada.

Fantasy Baseball © 1994 by Tim Scheidt

BÉISBOL DE FANTASÍA

Directiva para los jugadores

Usa las siguientes directivas para elegir los jugadores que quieres para formar tu equipo de béisbol. Aunque estas directivas no representan todo lo que debes considerar, te ayudarán cuando recibas la lista inicial de jugadores.

PROMEDIO DE BATEAR (AVG)

menos de .220 — bateador débil: no lo quieres a menos que las otras estadísticas (**OB%, HR:Cum. AB ratio, SO:Cum. AB ratio**) sean favorables.

.220 – .250 — un bateador ordinario: otra vez, revisa las otras estadísticas para evaluar las opciones.

.250 – .300 — un buen bateador, fiable; es muy probable que quieras quedarte con un jugador con esta capacidad menos que las otras estadísticas sean poco favorables o si estás listo para cambiarlo por otro beisbolista mejor.

más. de 300 — un bateador excelente: este puede llegar a ser tu superestrella. Puedes revisar las otras estadísticas pero es muy probable que quieras quedarte con este jugador.

PROMEDIO EN BASE

La opinion de un grupo de expertos estudiantiles:

> ***"A nosotros nos gustaría un jugador que tiene un promedio de 60-100 puntos más alto de estar en la base que su promedio de batear. También pensamos que el porcentaje debe de ser .340 o más alto. ¡Cuánto más alto sea el porcentaje mejor!"***

HR : CUM. AB (UNIDAD) RELACIÓN (RATIO)

Directivas para esta estadística sugeridas por los mismos expertos estudiantiles:

> ***"Consideramos un HR :Cum. AB ratio (relación) de 1:30 ser muy buena. Pensamos que esta relación u otra con números más chicas merece una buena consideración Por más chico el número que sea - mejor."***

SO : CUM. AB (UNIDAD) RELACIÓN (RATIO)

Directivas para esta estadística recomendadas por los mismos expertos estudiantiles:

> ***"Consideramos a una SO :Cum. AB promedio de 1:8 como muy buena. Pensamos que esta relación o una con el número más alto merece una consideración muy favorable. En este caso, ¡cuánto más alto sea el número mejor!***

BÉISBOL DE FANTASÍA

Tabla comparativa de jugadores

Nombre del equipo ______________________________

Directores ______________________________ ______________________________

Llena la tabla de abajo por cada jugador elegible que has recibido. Calcula el promedio de batear (AVG) y el porcentaje de llegar a la base al **milésimo** y apunta la HR:Cum. AB relación y SO:Cum. AB relación como unidades de relación aproximadas al **número entero** más próximo.

Pos./YR	Nombre	AB	Cum. AB	Avg.	OB%	HR : Cum. AB	SO : Cum. AB

Fantasy Baseball © 1994 by Tim Scheidt

Transparency Master

Robin Ventura Card

Height: 6'1" **Weight:** 192 lbs. **Bats:** Left **Throws:** Right **Born:** 7-14-67 Santa Maria, California

YR	TEAM	AVG	G	AB	R	H	2B	3B	HR	RBI	BB	SO	SB
89	WHITE SOX	.178	16	45	5	8	3	0	0	7	8	6	0
90	WHITE SOX	.249	150	493	48	123	17	1	5	54	55	53	1
91	WHITE SOX	.284	157	606	92	172	25	1	23	100	80	67	2
92	WHITE SOX	.282	157	592	85	167	38	1	16	93	93	71	2
4	**TOTALS**	.271	480	1736	230	470	83	3	44	254	236	197	5

Ventura won the American League Gold Glove at third base for the second consecutive year.

Upper Deck and the card/hologram combination are trademarks of The Upper Deck Company. © 1992 The Upper Deck Co. All Rights Reserved. Printed in the U.S.A.

Transparency Master

Actividad 1 Diario del director

Describe el mejor jugador que recibiste en la selección inicial. Usa la información estadística para defender tu selección.

Actividad 2 Diario del director

Escribe una carta que describa tu equipo de fantasía a un director de un equipo verdadero de la liga mayor (Tommy Lasorda, etc.) ¿Cuáles son las fuerzas de tu equipo? ¿Cuáles son sus debilidades? ¿Crees Que podrás competir con tu equipo durante la temporada? ¿Por qué sí o no? ¡Se creativo en la escritura!

Actividad 3 Diario del director

¿Explica el proceso que usaste para hacer el análisis estadístico completo de los jugadores de tu equipo. ¿Cómo puedes comprobar que tu análisis es correcto?

Fantasy Baseball © 1994 by Tim Scheidt

Transparency Master

Actividad 1 Evaluación de las actividades

Calculen el promedio de batear (AVG), el porcentaje de llegar a la base(OB), la culminación de los jonrónes (HR) : la relación para el número de batear(Cum. AB) y de ponchadas (SO) : la relación del número de bateos (AB) por cada jugador.

Actividad 3 Evaluación de las actividades

Analicen las estadísticas de este jugador, así cómo lo hicieron con sus propios equipos. Escriban un resumen del proceso que usaron para analizarlo.

Actividad 5 Evaluación de las actividades

Escriban una nueva Directiva para el bateo del pitcher que incremente, de una manera razonable, la posibilidad de resultados favorables. Escriban la relación y el porcentaje de los tiros : resultados posibles llegar a la base : resultados posibles, y fueras : resultados posibles. Escriban una descripción del proceso que usaron para crear la nueva directiva.

Transparency Master

Actividad 2 Preguntas y discusión

(La selección — ¿Cuáles son nuestras posibilidades?)

¿Qué probabilidad hay de recibir el primer jugador escogido en la selección? ¿Por qué piensas así?

¿Es ésta probabilidad la misma para todos los equipos? ¿Por qué so no?

Y si escogen primero tu tarjeta, ¿Aumenta o disminuye la posibilidad de que escojan tu tarjeta la vez siguiente?

¿Crees que es justo el sistema de lotería que usan para escoger jugadores en la seleccíon de libre agencia? Explica por qué sí o no y que cambiarías para mejorar el sistema.

Fantasy Baseball © 1994 by Tim Scheidt

BÉISBOL DE FANTASÍA

Directivas estadísticas

Esta directiva se presenta con la intención de usarla como un recurso para llenar la **Tabla analítica de jugadores** para cada uno de tus jugadores. Para llenar las tablas se encontrarás todas las estadísticas necesarias detrás de las tarjetas de béisbol.

* Para determinar el **número acumulado de tiros (Cum. AB)** — suma todas las veces que estaba por batear (AB) al número de veces de llegar a la base con bolas (BB) que se encuentran detrás de la tarjeta.

* Para determinar **los sencillos (1B)** — quita (resta) el número de dobles (2B), triples (3B) y jonrones (HR) del número de golpes(H) que se muestran detrás de la tarjeta.

* Para determinar las **Otras fueras** — suma los golpes (H), bases en bolas (BB) y ponchadas (SO) y quita el total de la Cum. AB.

* Para determinar **Fueras por el aire (FO)** y **Fueras por el suelo (GO)** — divide el número de **Otras fueras** por 2. Pon el cociente debajo de las dos entradas **(FO)** and **(GO)**.

$$\textbf{Ejemplo:}\quad \frac{\textbf{Otras fueras}}{\textbf{142}} \qquad \frac{\textbf{142}}{\textbf{2}} \qquad \frac{\textbf{FO}}{\textbf{71}} \qquad \frac{\textbf{GO}}{\textbf{71}}$$

(Si el número de Otras Fueras es impar, solo suma 1 antes de dividir por 2.)

* Para representar la relación de las estadísticas acumuladas de AB como una fracción — anota el total Cum. AB como el denominador y el valor de cada estadística como el **numerador**.

* Para determinar el Equivalente decimal — divide el numerador por el denominador. Sólo anota hasta el cuarto decimal.

$$\textbf{Ejemplo:}\quad \frac{\textbf{1B}}{\textbf{Cum. AB}} = \frac{\textbf{109}}{\textbf{551}} = \textbf{.1978}$$

* Para determinar los **Grados** — multiplica el equivalente decimal de cada estadística por 360 (número de grados en un círculo). Redondea el producto al número entero más cercano.

Ejemplo: .1978 x 360 = 71.208 o 71 grados

BÉISBOL DE FANTASÍA

Tabla analítica del jugador

(Ejemplos)

AÑO 1991

Nombre	Cum. AB	H	1B	2B	3B	HR	BB	SO	Otras Fueras	FO	GO
Robin Ventura	686	172	123	25	1	23	80	67	367	183	184
RELACIÓN			$\frac{123}{686}$	$\frac{25}{686}$	$\frac{1}{686}$	$\frac{23}{686}$	$\frac{80}{686}$	$\frac{67}{686}$		$\frac{183}{686}$	$\frac{184}{686}$
EQUIVALENTE DECIMAL			.1793	.0364	.0014	.0335	.1166	.0976		.2667	.2682
GRADOS			65°	13°	0°	12°	42°	35°		96°	97°

AÑO 1985

Nombre	Cum. AB	H	1B	2B	3B	HR	BB	SO	Otras Fueras	FO	GO
Willie McGee	646	216	162	26	18	10	34	86	310	155	155
RELACIÓN			$\frac{162}{646}$	$\frac{26}{646}$	$\frac{18}{646}$	$\frac{10}{646}$	$\frac{34}{646}$	$\frac{86}{646}$		$\frac{155}{646}$	$\frac{155}{646}$
EQUIVALENTE DECIMAL			.2508	.0402	.0279	.0155	.0526	.1331		.2399	.2399
GRADOS			90°	14°	10°	6°	19°	48°		86°	86°

Fantasy Baseball © 1994 by Tim Scheidt

BÉISBOL DE FANTASÍA

Tabla analítica del jugador

AÑO______

Nombre	Cum. AB	H	1B	2B	3B	HR	BB	SO	Otras Fueras	FO	GO
RELACIÓN											
EQUIVALENTE DECIMAL											
GRADOS											

AÑO______

Nombre	Cum. AB	H	1B	2B	3B	HR	BB	SO	Otras Fueras	FO	GO
RELACIÓN											
EQUIVALENTE DECIMAL											
GRADOS											

Nombre ______________________________

Fecha ______________________________

Período _______

PROBLEMA AVANZADO #1

¡Agárralo - Si puedes!

Usualmente, Speed Durgan tarda 3.4 segundos en recorrer los noventa(90) pies que separan una base de la otra. Bull McKinley, pitcher, tira la pelota a 84 m.p.h. Rich Crowe, catcher, le han cronometrado el tiro de jon a la segunda base en 70 m.p.h. Normalmente Rich tarda 1.3 segundos para soltar la pelota que le tiró Bull.

Si Speed está adelantado 3 pies de la primera base y empieza a correr hacia la segunda base precisamente al mismo tiempo que Bull suelta la pelota, ¿llegará Speed a la segunda base a tiempo o quedará fuera? Usa tus cálculos y cualquier otro factor que consideres importante para demostrar tu conclusión.

*** La distancia del pitcher a jon es de 60'6".**

Fantasy Baseball © 1994 by Tim Scheidt

BÉISBOL DE FANTASÍA

Problema semanal (P.O.W.) Procedimiento

Usa el siguiente procedimiento P.O.W. para encontrar la solución a los problemas planteados. Anota la información en una hoja separada.

1. **ENUNCIA EL PROBLEMA** Escribe el enunciado del problema con una o más oraciones completas. Además, describe la estrategía inicial que usaste para empezar el trabajo.

2. **HAZ EL TRABAJO** Incluye dibujos, los cálculos, tablas, ecuaciones cualquier otro método que usaste para resolverlo.

3. **DECLARA TU SOLUCIÓN** Escríbela en una o más oraciones completas.

4. **EXPLICA TU RAZONAMIENTO** En uno o más párrafos, explica porqué crees que tu solución es razonable. Asegúrate que te refieres al trabajo(#2) cuando quieras justificar el razonamiento de tu solución.

Transparency Master

Actividad 3 Preguntas y discusión

(¿Cómo se pueden usar las estadísticas de los jugadores?)

¿Qué información se encuentra en la rueda y detrás dr las tarjetas de béisbol? ¿Qué información se encuentra en las ruedas que no están en las tarjetas? ¿Cómo conseguiste esta información?

Con la información de las tarjetas, ¿Cómo puedes determinar las veces que un jugador ha bateado? Recuerda que las BB (base en bolas) no se incluyen en el número de bateos (AB) de las tarjetas. ¿Cómo te puede ayudar esta información en la construcción de las ruedas?

¿Cómo se puede representar cada estadística en las tarjetas como una fracción? ¿Que parte de la fracción representa cada estadística?

¿Se pueden usar estas fracciones para construir las ruedas? ¿Cómo puedes encontrar el decimal o el porcentaje equivalente de estas fracciones? ¿Cómo se puede usar esta información?

¿Cuál es la relación entre un porcentaje y una fracción? ¿Qué es el denominador de una representación fraccional de 17%?

¿Qué unidad de medir se usa para medir los círculos? ¿Es importante saber esto para llenar tus ruedas estadísticas correctamente? ¿Por qué sí o no?

¿Con cuanta precisión se deben hacer los cálculos? ¿Por qué es importante tener cierto nivel de precisión?

Fantasy Baseball © 1994 by Tim Scheidt

BÉISBOL DE FANTASIA

Cómo construir la rueda de jugador

AÑO 1991

Nombre	Cum. AB	H	1B	2B	3B	HR	BB	SO	Otras Fueras	FO	GO
Robin Ventura	686	172	123	25	1	23	80	67	367	183	184
RELACIÓN			123/686	25/686	1/686	23/686	80/686	67/686		183/686	184/686
EQUIVALENTE DECIMAL			.1793	.0364	.0014	.0335	.1166	.0976		.2667	.2682
GRADOS			65°	13°	0°	12°	42°	35°		96°	97°

A. Usa la copia de la **Rueda de jugador** o haz 2 círculos de 4 $^1/_2$" de diámetro en cartulina. Marca con claridad el punto central de los dos círculos.

B. Usa el transportador para dibujar el radio derecho en la rueda.

C. Decide en que órden quieres poner las categorías estadísticas. Con tu primera categoría haz el ángulo apropiado y dibuja otros radios. Clasifica esta sección con la abreviatura estadistica correcta.

D. Sigue con el **paso** (C) hasta medir todos los ángulos y escribir todas las abreviaturas estadísticas.

E. Escribe el nombre completo del jugador detrás de la rueda.

F. Recorta la rueda.

G. Recorta otra rueda de una cartulina de otro color a lo ancho en dos piezas iguales. Estas servirán como la base de la rueda.

H.
- Si vas a usar las flechas transparentes, centra la rueda y pégala con goma a la base.
- Si vas a hacer flechas con las ruedas, sigue la direcciones que se encuentran en la hoja **Hacer Flechas.**

I. Decora la base de la rueda de jugador. Se creativo. Incluye el nombre, posición, nombre del equipo, y su promedio de batear en la base de la rueda.

BÉISBOL DE FANTASÍA

Cómo hacer una rueda de jugador

(modelo pictórico)

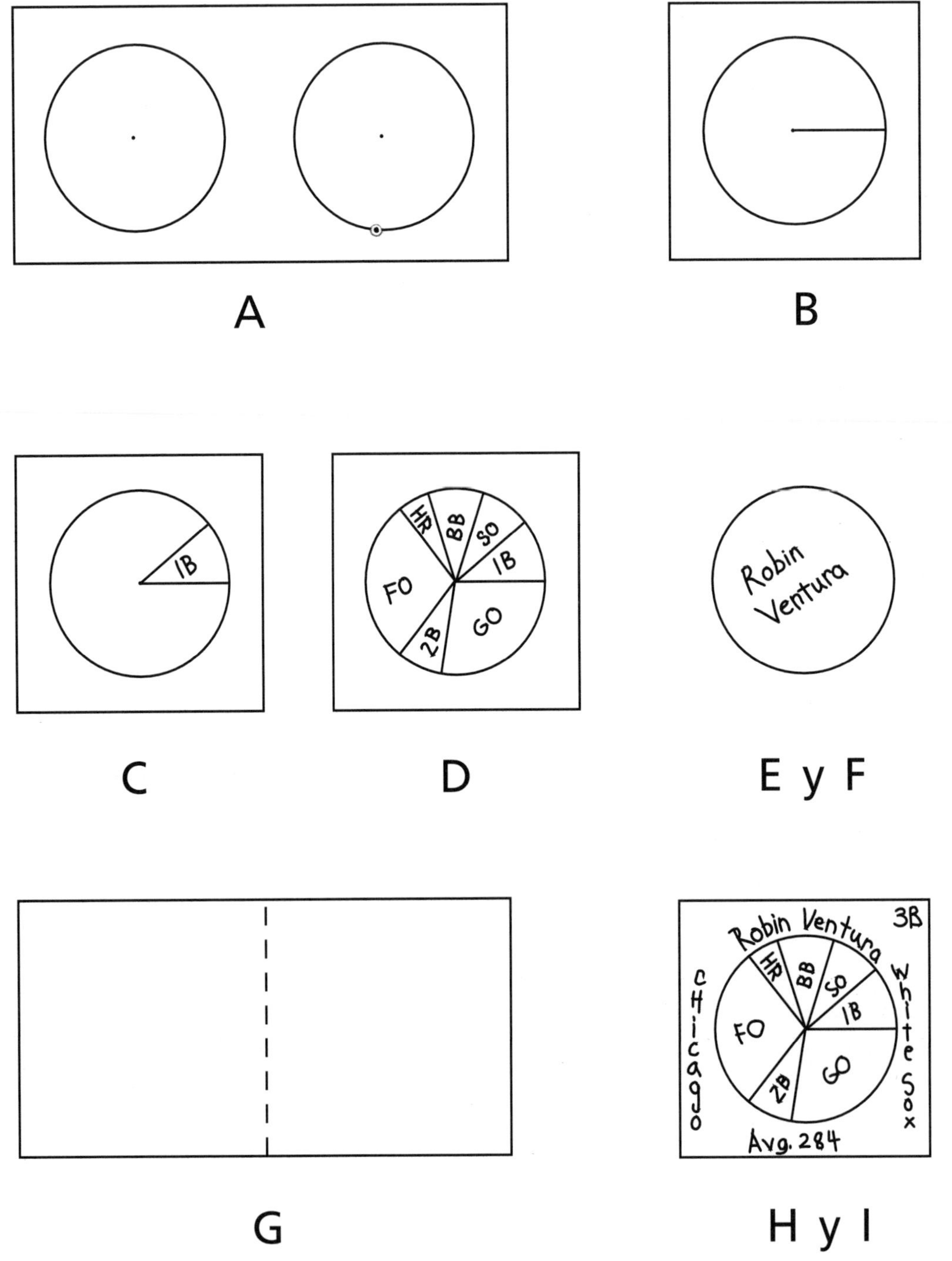

 Fantasy Baseball © 1994 by Tim Scheidt

BÉISBOL DE FANTASÍA

Hacer Flechas

1. Calcula aproximadamente el centro de la base y marca un punto claro en el centro. Usa una regla para trazar una línea negra fina y recta desde el punto central hasta la esquina izquierda de abajo.

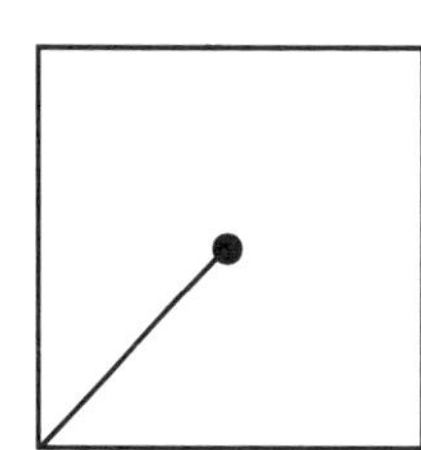

2. Recorta tres cuadrados de 1" por 1" de la cartulina que usaste para las ruedas.

3. Dobla el sujetepapeles para que la curva chica de adentro sobresalga. Jala la punta de esta curva para enderezarla. Usa esta punta para hacer agujeros en el centro de la rueda y de la base.

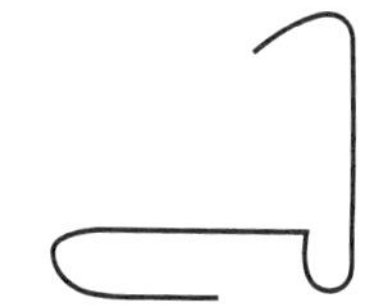

4. Mete el sujetepapeles doblado por el agujero de la base (va por debajo hacia arriba). La curva grande del sujetepapeles debe quedar plana debajo de la base.

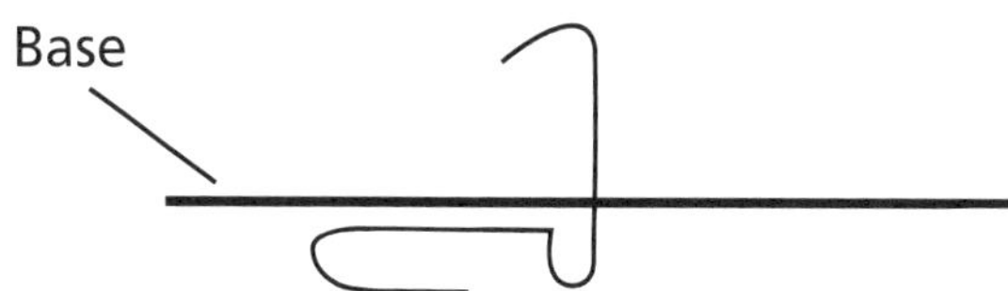

5. Pon los tres cuadrados de papel y la rueda sobre el sujetepapeles encima de la base. Dobla el sujetepapeles por abajo.

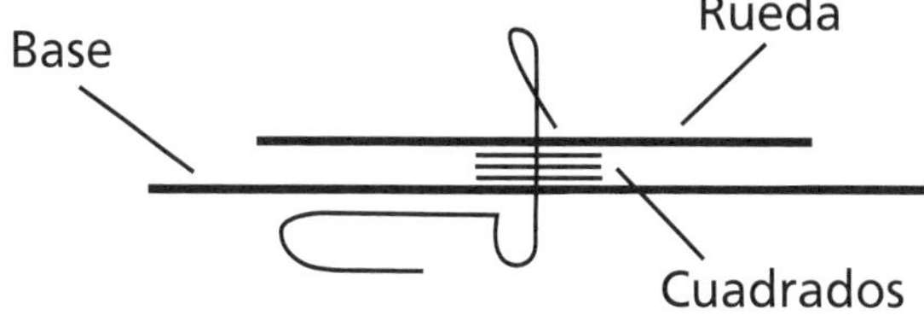

6. Pega el sujetapapeles a la base con cinta adhesiva.

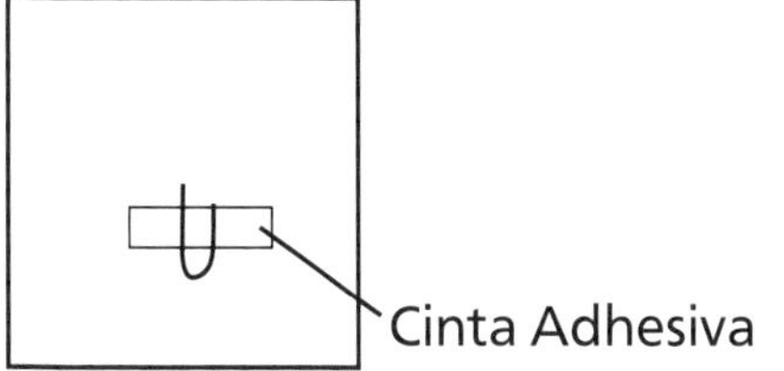

Rueda de jugador

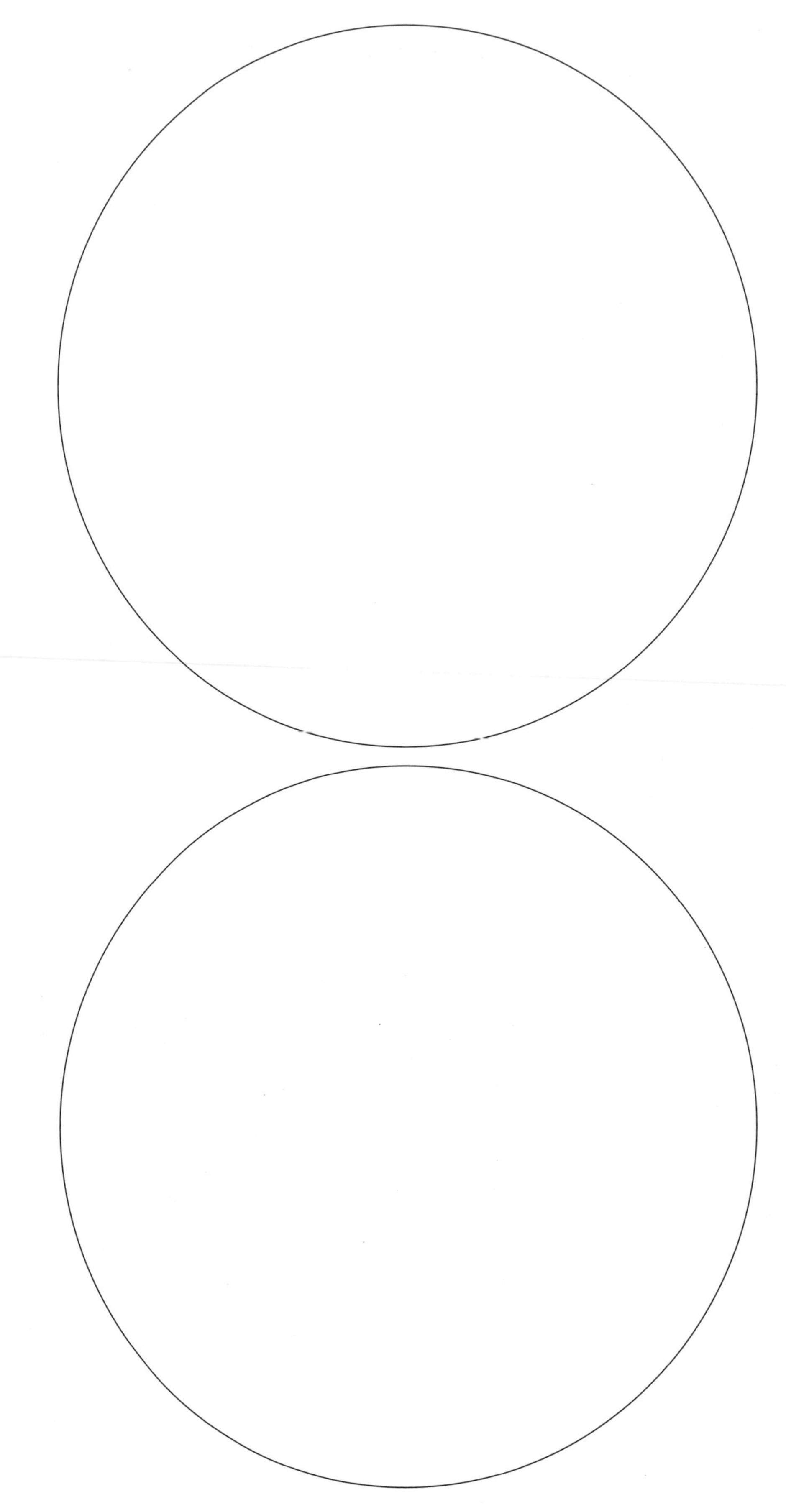

Transparency Master

Actividad 4 Diario del director

Mi impresión de Béisbol de fantasía hasta hoy es . . .

Actividad 5 Diario del director

Describe lo que has descubierto en tu investigación de la directiva para el bateo del pitcher? ¿Cómo usarás la información para jugar el juego real?

Actividad 6 Diario del director

En unos pocos días empezarás el primer partido de la temporada regular. Escribe una carta al Director General (GM) de tu equipo, haz una lista con el órden de batear que piensas usar en el primer juego. Usa las estadísticas para defender el órden en que has colocado a los jugadores.

BÉISBOL DE FANTASÍA

Directivas para tantos

Esta directiva se usa para contestar las preguntas sobre tantos que se les puedan ocurrir durante un juego. Esta directiva no se propone tratar las situaciones individuales que puedan ocurrir en un juego verdadero, sino proveerles una norma consistente para todos los juegos de Béisbol de fantasía.

SI LA PERSONA QUE BATEA RECIBE UN . . .	LOS JUGADORES QUE ESTÁN EN BASE . . .
• Sencillo (1B)	avanza una base.
• Doble (2B)	avanza dos bases.
• Triple (3B)	todos llegan a jon.
• Jonrón (HR)	todos llegan a jon.
• Base con bolas (BB)	avanza una base sólo si hay necesidad de mover el bateador a la primera base.
• Ponchada (SO)	no se avanza
• Fuera por el aire (FO)	no se avanza a menos que haya un jugador en la 3er base y haya menos de 2 fueras. En estas circunstancias, él que está en el 3er base hace un punto.
• Fuera por el suelo (GO)	avanza una base a menos que hayan dos fueras en la entrada.

Fantasy Baseball © 1994 by Tim Scheidt

BÉISBOL DE FANTASÍA

Directivas para el bateo del pitcher

Cuando le toque batear, usarás dados porque no tienes una rueda para él. Todas las posibilidades que hay para la suma de los dos dados se encuentran abajo. Marca los resultados de batear de tu pitcher de la misma manera que lo haces para los otros jugadores.

SI TIRAS UNA SUMA DE . . .	TU PITCHER RECIBE UN. . .
2	doble (2B)
3	sencillo(1B)
4	ponchada (SO)
5	base por bolas (BB)
6	fuera por el aire(FO)
7	ponchada (SO)
8	fuera por el suelo (GO)
9	ponchada (SO)
10	fuera por el aire (FO)
11	sencillo (1B)
12	jonrón (HR)

_____ CONTRA _____ EN _____ TANTEADOR _____ FECHA _____

Tanteo por inning	1	2	3	4	5	6	7	8	9	10

Tanteo Final	

Nombre	POS	1	2	3	4	5	6	7	8	9	10	AB	R	H	2B	3B	HR	BB	SO	RBI
		BB 1B 2B 3B HR	BB 1B 2B 3B HR	BB 1B 2B 3B HR	BB 1B 2B 3B HR	BB 1B 2B 3B HR	BB 1B 2B 3B HR	BB 1B 2B 3B HR	BB 1B 2B 3B HR	BB 1B 2B 3B HR	BB 1B 2B 3B HR									
		BB 1B 2B 3B HR	BB 1B 2B 3B HR	BB 1B 2B 3B HR	BB 1B 2B 3B HR	BB 1B 2B 3B HR	BB 1B 2B 3B HR	BB 1B 2B 3B HR	BB 1B 2B 3B HR	BB 1B 2B 3B HR	BB 1B 2B 3B HR									
		BB 1B 2B 3B HR	BB 1B 2B 3B HR	BB 1B 2B 3B HR	BB 1B 2B 3B HR	BB 1B 2B 3B HR	BB 1B 2B 3B HR	BB 1B 2B 3B HR	BB 1B 2B 3B HR	BB 1B 2B 3B HR	BB 1B 2B 3B HR									
		BB 1B 2B 3B HR	BB 1B 2B 3B HR	BB 1B 2B 3B HR	BB 1B 2B 3B HR	BB 1B 2B 3B HR	BB 1B 2B 3B HR	BB 1B 2B 3B HR	BB 1B 2B 3B HR	BB 1B 2B 3B HR	BB 1B 2B 3B HR									
		BB 1B 2B 3B HR	BB 1B 2B 3B HR	BB 1B 2B 3B HR	BB 1B 2B 3B HR	BB 1B 2B 3B HR	BB 1B 2B 3B HR	BB 1B 2B 3B HR	BB 1B 2B 3B HR	BB 1B 2B 3B HR	BB 1B 2B 3B HR									
		BB 1B 2B 3B HR	BB 1B 2B 3B HR	BB 1B 2B 3B HR	BB 1B 2B 3B HR	BB 1B 2B 3B HR	BB 1B 2B 3B HR	BB 1B 2B 3B HR	BB 1B 2B 3B HR	BB 1B 2B 3B HR	BB 1B 2B 3B HR									
		BB 1B 2B 3B HR	BB 1B 2B 3B HR	BB 1B 2B 3B HR	BB 1B 2B 3B HR	BB 1B 2B 3B HR	BB 1B 2B 3B HR	BB 1B 2B 3B HR	BB 1B 2B 3B HR	BB 1B 2B 3B HR	BB 1B 2B 3B HR									
		BB 1B 2B 3B HR	BB 1B 2B 3B HR	BB 1B 2B 3B HR	BB 1B 2B 3B HR	BB 1B 2B 3B HR	BB 1B 2B 3B HR	BB 1B 2B 3B HR	BB 1B 2B 3B HR	BB 1B 2B 3B HR	BB 1B 2B 3B HR									
		BB 1B 2B 3B HR	BB 1B 2B 3B HR	BB 1B 2B 3B HR	BB 1B 2B 3B HR	BB 1B 2B 3B HR	BB 1B 2B 3B HR	BB 1B 2B 3B HR	BB 1B 2B 3B HR	BB 1B 2B 3B HR	BB 1B 2B 3B HR									
		BB 1B 2B 3B HR	BB 1B 2B 3B HR	BB 1B 2B 3B HR	BB 1B 2B 3B HR	BB 1B 2B 3B HR	BB 1B 2B 3B HR	BB 1B 2B 3B HR	BB 1B 2B 3B HR	BB 1B 2B 3B HR	BB 1B 2B 3B HR									
Totales de Equipos																				

Fantasy Baseball © 1994 by Tim Scheidt

Mets **CONTRA** Tigers **EN** Tiger Stadium **TANTEADOR** ________ **FECHA** 7-16-93

Tanteo por Inning

	1	2	3	4	5	6	7	8	9	10
	0	0	3	1	0	2	0	0	1	
	1	1	2	0	7	0	0	2	/	

Tanteo Final

Mets	7
Tigers	13

Nombre	POS	1	2	3	4	5	~~6~~ 5	~~7~~ 6	~~8~~ 7	~~9~~ 8	~~10~~ 9	AB	R	H	2B	3B	HR	BB	SO	RBI
Greg Gagne	SS	FO (1)	1B RBI		GO (2)	BB		K (3)		GO (3)		5	1	1	0	0	0	1	1	1
Terry Pendleton	3B	2B	GO (3)		FO (3)	HR 4 RBI's			FO (1)			5	2	2	1	0	1	0	0	4
Bo Jackson	OF	BB		2B		1B	1B		FO (2)			4	2	3	1	0	0	1	0	0
Kirby Puckett	OF	GO (2)		GO (1)		1B	BB		GO (3)			4	1	1	0	0	0	1	0	0
Hal Morris	1B	1B RBI		RBI SF (2)		1B	GO (3)			3B		4	2	3	0	1	0	0	0	2
Kevin McReynolds	OF	K (3)		HR RBI		BB RBI		FO (1)		HR 2 RBI's		4	3	2	0	0	2	1	1	4
Joe Girardi	C		FO (1)	BB		RBI SF (1)		1B		K (1)		3	0	1	0	0	0	1	1	1
Lance Blankenship	2B		3B	K (3)		2B RBI		GO (2)		BB		4	2	2	1	1	0	1	1	1
Nolan Ryan	P		K (2)		GO (1)	K (2)		BB		K (2)		4	0	0	0	0	0	1	3	0
Totales de Equipo												37	13	16	4	2	3	7	7	13

Transparency Master

Actividad 5 Preguntas y discusión

(Investigar las directivas para el bateo del pitcher)

Cuando uno batea, ¿Cuál es el porcentaje de posibilidades de darle a la bola y llegar a la base? Compara este porcentaje con el porcentaje de otras posibilidades.

Cuál es la relación de llegar a la base (por tiros, bolas, etc.) en comparación con todas las otras posibilidades? ¿Cuál es el porcentaje?

¿Cuál es la relación de hacer un tiro fuera con todas las posibilidades cuando uno batea? ¿Cuál es el porcentaje?

¿La suma de estas tres porcentajes llega a ser 100%? ¿Por qué sí o no?

¿Crees que el pitcher tiene buenas posibilidades de lleguar a la base? ¿Por qué sí o no?

 Fantasy Baseball © 1994 by Tim Scheidt

Nombre ______________________________

Fechas ______________________________

Período _______

PROBLEMA AVANZADO #2

Uniformes llamativos

Para promover la asistencia del público a tus próximos juegos, has decidido comprar uniformes de colores llamativos para tu equipo. Piensas que cuanto más llamativos sean los uniformes, más interés tendrá el público. El problema es que no sabes ¿qué combinación de colores debes usar?

Sabes que tienes que comprar los siguientes artículos de ropa para los jugadores:
camisa, pantalones, estribos de calcetín, zapatos y **gorras.**

Puedes escoger de los siguientes colores:
negro, blanco, durazno, aquamarino, rojo, azul, y **anaranjado**

Para cumplir con las directivas de la liga, tienes que seguir las siguientes instrucciones:

- Las camisas tienen que llevar **tres** colores diferentes.
- Los pantalones tienen que llevar **dos** colores diferentes.
- Los estribos de calcetín deben ser de **un** color.
- Los zapatos llevan **dos** colores y los cordones son de un color diferente de los dos colores de los zapatos.
- La gorra debe tener **tres** colores diferentes.

Si sigues las reglas, ¿Cuántas combinaciones hay para hacer un uniforme completo?

** Usa una de las combinaciones posibles para diseñar y dibujar un uniforme para tu equipo.

BÉISBOL DE FANTASÍA

Hoja de estadísticas del equipo

Director____________________ Director____________________

Equipo____________________

Nombre	AB	R	H	2B	3B	HR	BB	SO	RBI	AVG.	OB%	SLG. %

Fantasy Baseball © 1994 by Tim Scheidt

BÉISBOL DE FANTASÍA

Muestras de los programas

LUNES	MARTES	MIÉRCOLES
Yankees vs. Padres	Yankees vs. Phillies	Yankees vs. Tigers
Tigers vs. Giants	Tigers vs. Mets	Orioles vs. Angels
Angels vs. Phillies	Angels vs. Padres	Padres vs. Giants
Orioles vs. Mets	Orioles vs. Giants	Phillies vs. Mets
Yankees vs. Giants	Yankees vs. Mets	Yankees vs. Angels
Tigers vs. Phillies	Tigers vs. Padres	Orioles vs. Tigers
Angels vs. Mets	Angels vs. Giants	Phillies vs. Padres
Orioles vs. Padres	Orioles vs. Phillies	Giants vs. Mets

LUNES	MARTES	MIÉRCOLES	NÚMEROS/EQUIPOS
1 vs. 8	1 vs. 6	1 vs. 4	1 - Yankees
2 vs. 7	2 vs. 5	2 vs. 3	2 - Tigers
3 vs. 6	3 vs. 8	5 vs. 8	3 - Angels
4 vs. 5	4 vs. 7	6 vs. 7	4 - Orioles
			5 - Padres
1 vs. 7	1 vs. 5	1 vs. 3	6 - Giants
2 vs. 6	2 vs. 8	2 vs. 4	7 - Phillies
3 vs. 5	3 vs. 7	5 vs. 7	8 - Mets
4 vs. 8	4 vs. 6	6 vs. 8	

BÉISBOL DE FANTASÍA

Tarea — Programa regular de la temporada

Crea con tu compañero, un **programa regular de la temporada–Béisbol de fantasía** para 10 días que se pueda usar con la clase. Tu programa debe ser fácil para leer y debe de incluir lo siguiente:

- Cada equipo tiene que jugar con todos los equipos al menos una vez.
- Cada equipo juega 20 partidos.
- Cada equipo juega el mísmo número de partidos en su estadio local.

Se deben usar los diez períodos de clase para crear el programa en los días que tu maestro indica como días para jugar Beísbol de fantasía. Acúerdate que todos los equipos deben jugar dos partidos diarios.

Si la cantidad de equipos de tu clase es impar, uno de ellos recibirá un "descanso" (BYE) en cada vuelta de juegos. Cuando un equipo tiene un BYE (descanso), automaticamente recibe una victoria porque está jugando contra sí mismo. Ningún equipo debe recibir más que dos descansos en tu programa.

*** **AVISO IMPORTANTE: Los que copien creativamente su programa final en un cartulina grande, serán incluídos en la elección para ver qué Programa de béisbol de fantasía usarán con toda la clase.**

Fantasy Baseball © 1994 by Tim Scheidt

Transparency Master

Actividad 6 Preguntas y discusión

(Posición de los jugadores — ¿Qué importancia tiene?)

Revisa tu hoja de estadísticas. ¿Todos tus jugadores batean la misma cantidad de veces? ¿Qué jugadores batean más, los que están al principio o a lo ultimo de la lista? ¿Hay una diferencia significante? Según las estadísticas, ¿quieres que ciertos jugadores bateen más que otros?

¿En qué posición pondrías a un jugador que tenga un alto promedio de batear? ¿Dónde va el jugador con un alto porcentaje de llegar a la base? ¿Cómo afecta al juego el orden de los bateadores?

¿En qué lugar se debe poner a un jugador que batea jonrones? ¿Por qué sería productivo este lugar?

¿Cómo se comparan las estadísticas de tus pitcheres con las de otros jugadores? Si son más bajas, ¿por qué será? Si son casi iguales, ¿será necesario poner a los pitcheres al final de la lista? ¿Por qué sí o no?

Transparency Master

Actividad 6 Preguntas y discusión

(Revisar la posición de los jugadores)

En tu hoja de estadísticas tienes tres maneras de medir estadísticas: Promedio (Avg.), En Base (OB%) y el Bateo Fuerte (Slg. %). Haz una lista particular de cada estadística, comienza con el mejor jugador y continúa con los otros jugadores en órden descendiente.

¿En qué posición a un jugador que tiene el mejor promedio de batear con fuerza (Slg. %)?

¿Crees que las estadísticas de los cinco juegos representan con precisión los resultados de los jugadores después de 40 - 50 juegos en la temporada? ¿Por qué sí o no? ¿Hay más información que se debe considerar antes de hacer la lista de batear? Si hay, ¿dónde se encuentra esta información?

Fantasy Baseball © 1994 by Tim Scheidt

Transparency Master

Actividad 6 Evaluación de las actividades

¿Dónde pondrías a estos dos jugadores? Defiende tu decisión con estadísticas.

Actividad 8 Evaluación de las actividades

Respondan a la situación presentada abajo usando los diagramas, gráficas, ruedas, escritura, etc. para explicar tu razonamiento:

Estás en la última entrada del juego (la novena) y empataron 3 a 3. Tus jugadores se encuentran en la primera y en la segunda base, con dos fueras, y le toca batear a tu pitcher. Tienes dos posibilidades, dejar batear a tu pitcher o que el jugador en la tercera base robe a jon (el juega en la posición de segundo en tu equipo). ¿Qué vas a hacer? Defiende tu decisión con datos matemáticos.

Nombre ______________________________

Fecha ______________________________

Período _______

BÉISBOL DE FANTASÍA

La probabilidad teórica vs. la experimental

¿Qué pasará si (teórica). . .

Nombre	Cum. AB	H	1B	2B	3B	HR	BB	SO	Otras Fueras	FO	GO
RELACIÓN											
EQUIVALENTE DECIMAL											
GRADOS											
PROBABILIDAD TEÓRICA (360 VUELTAS)											

Mi predicción antes de dar 360 vueltas es. . .

Nombre	Cum. AB	H	1B	2B	3B	HR	BB	SO	Otras Fueras	FO	GO
	360										

Los resultados después de dar 360 vueltas son (experimental) . . .

Nombre	Cum. AB	H	1B	2B	3B	HR	BB	SO	Otras Fueras	FO	GO
	360										

Fantasy Baseball © 1994 by Tim Scheidt

Transparency Master

Actividad 7 Diario del director

En tus propias palabras, explica lo que has hecho en clase estos últimos días y lo que has aprendido. Incluye todo lo que aprendiste sobre las probabilidades.

Actividad 8 Diario del director

Escribe un artículo para el periódico que ponga al día lo que ha pasado con tu equipo. ¿Cuál es tu récord? ¿Cómo van los jugadores particulares? ¿Has hecho recientemente alguna decisión como director que haya ayudado al equipo? ¿Cómo se ve el futuro de los próximos vinco juegos?

Actividad 9 Diario del director

Escribe uno o dos párrafos por cada uno de tus tres jugadores, compara las estadísticas de las tarjetas con las estadísticas que conseguiste durante la temporada regular. Usa las tablas completas como un recurso para hacer una comparación precisa de las estadisticas.

BÉISBOL DE FANTASÍA

Tabla de posiciones de los equipos/líderes por promedio

(Muestras)

BÉISBOL DE FANTASÍA
TABLA DE POSICIONES DE LOS EQUIPOS

Liga Norteamericana				Liga Nacional			
EQUIPO	W	L	PCT.	EQUIPO	W	L	PCT.
Tigers	5	0	1.000	Cardinals	4	1	.800
Orioles	4	1	.800	Padres	4	1	.800
Twins	4	1	.800	Giants	3	2	.600
Royals	3	2	.600	Expos	2	3	.400
Yankees	3	2	.600	Mets	1	4	.200
Indians	2	3	.400	Cubs	0	5	.000
Rangers	0	5	.000	Dodgers	0	5	.000

BÉISBOL DE FANTASÍA
LÍDERES DEL PROMEDIO DE BATEAR

NOMBRE	EQUIPO	PROMEDIO
Lou Whitaker	Tigers	.583
Will Clark	Mets	.514
Wade Boggs	Indians	.474
Frank Thomas	Twins	.459
Andre Dawson	Giants	.406
Barry Bonds	Cardinals	.388
Ken Griffey Jr.	Cardinals	.372
Gary Sheffield	Orioles	.351
Tony Gwynn	Rangers	.349
Paul Molitor	Padres	.333

Fantasy Baseball © 1994 by Tim Scheidt

Nombre ______________________________

Fecha ______________________________

Período _______

PROBLEMA AVANZADO #3

Aumento de salarios — 2000

En 1981, Dave Winfield de los Yankees de Nueva York, recibió un contrato récord por 2.2 millones de dólares al año. En 1992, Ryne Sandberg de los Cubs de Chicago, firmó un contrato que le garantizaba un salario promedio de 7.1 millones de dólares al año.

Usa lo que sabes de crecimiento económico para hacer lo siguiente:

- Determina el factor de crecimiento con el modelo de sumar y el modelo de multiplicar para estos salarios. Con los factores de crecimiento respectivos, trata de predecir el máximo salario posible en el año 2000.

- Escribe una carta al Comisario de béisbol a favor en o contra del aumento de los salarios. No te olvides de usar tus predicciónes matemáticas para defender tu decisión.

Fantasy Baseball © 1994 by Tim Scheidt

Transparency Master

Actividad 8 Preguntas y discusión

(Después de 5 juegos — Investigación sobre bases robadas)

¿Tienen todos los todos los jugadores la misma habilidad para robar bases?

¿Deben tener todos la misma oportunidad de éxito?

¿Son algunas bases más fáciles de robar que otras?

¿Pueden dos o más jugadores robar la misma base a la vez?

¿Puede un jugador robar más de una base a la vez?

¿Hay algunas bases que no se pueden robar?

¿Hay alguna situación en que no se puede robar la base?

¿Cómo se puede usar la información que hay detrás de las tarjetas para crear nuestro propio método?

Fantasy Baseball © 1994 by Tim Scheidt

Transparency Master

Culminación del estudio Preguntas y discusión

(Actividad final — diario del director)

Si tuvieras que empezar una nueva temporada de Béisbol de fantasía, ¿te quedarías con la misma rueda o harías unas nuevas con las estadísticas más recientes?

Si tus jugadores tendrían que jugar 25 partidos más, ¿crees que sus estadísticas serían mejores o peores? Defiende tu respuesta.

Después ee jugar 20 juegos enla temporada regular del Béisbol de fantasía, ¿Crees que es importante el lugar donde de ponen las categorías? ¿Por qué sí o no?

Si tuvieras que crear nuevamente las ruedas de jugadores, ¿usarías las mismas estadísticas u otras diferentes? ¿Cómo lo harías?

Nombre______________________________

Fecha ______________________________

Período_______

EVALUACIÓN INDIVIDUAL

Acuerdo de libre agencia

Dos nuevos jugadores son elegibles para la selección en la libre agencia de Béisbol de fantasía. Abajo se encuentran las estadísticas de los últimos años de servicio. Analiza estas estadísticas para determinar qué jugador escogerías para tu equipo. Defiende tu selección con la información estadística.

JUGADOR A

AB	H	2B	3B	HR	BB	SO
489	161	31	3	7	97	48

JUGADOR B

AB	H	2B	3B	HR	BB	SO
619	186	42	2	32	87	114

¿A quién escogerîas, al jugador A o al Jugador B? ¿Por qué?

Fantasy Baseball © 1994 by Tim Scheidt

PROYECTO BÉISBOL DE FANTASÍA

Una evaluación abierta

Situación:
Tú y tu compañero han sido contratados como consultores por una gran empresa editorial. El editor de la empresa ha oído algo de un estudio **Béisbol de fantasía** y quiere conocer sus opiniones para saber más sobre este estudio. Si convencen a la empresa que el estudio vale la pena, lo publicará y venderá con el nombre de la empresa. A la empresa le preocupan dos cuestiones:

1. Quiere asegurarse que el estudio contiene suficiente matemáticas adecuada para los estudiantes que participan en el estudio.

2. Quiere asegurarse que los estudiantes tienen la oportunidad de comunicarse con sus compañeros y de usar su creatividad durante su participación en el estudio.

Acuérdense que los directores de la empresa saben muy poco del estudio y por eso los contrataron a ustedes.

Su tarea
Creen una exhibición para explicar que es el estudio de **Béisbol de fantasía**. La exhibición deberá incluir muestras, ilustraciones, descripciones escritas, etc. — y cualquier otra cosa que le ayudará al editor entender mejor el estudio. No se olviden de los dos criterios mencionados anteriormente. Tal vez quieran incluir más información de tu propio equipo de **Béisbol de fantasía** en la exhibición.

Preparen una presentación de 3-5 minutos para la Mesa directiva. Presenten la información que necesitan los directores para que se decidan a publicar el estudio o no. La Mesa directiva los evaluará según la claridad de la presentación, además de la exhibición visual y escrita.

Director(es):____

PROYECTO BÉISBOL DE FANTASÍA

Comentarios de la mesa directiva

Presentación:____

Exhibición:____

- -

Director(es):____

PROYECTO BÉISBOL DE FANTASÍA

Comentarios de la mesa directiva

Presentación:____

Exhibición:____

Fantasy Baseball © 1994 by Tim Scheidt

NOTES

NOTES